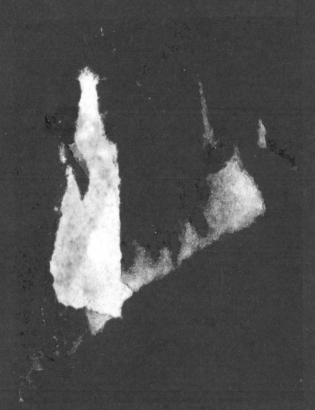

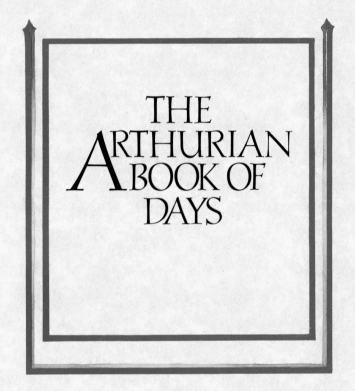

THE ARTHURIAN BOOK OF DAYS

To Emrys:
his first Arthurian retelling,
with pictures, of course.

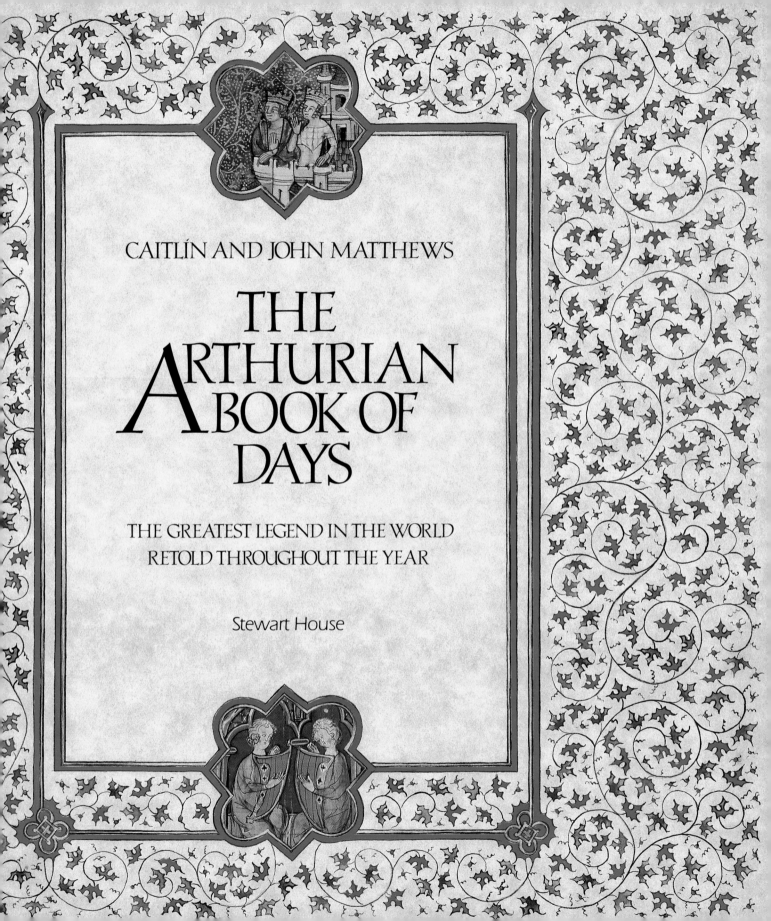

CAITLÍN AND JOHN MATTHEWS

THE ARTHURIAN
A BOOK OF
DAYS

THE GREATEST LEGEND IN THE WORLD
RETOLD THROUGHOUT THE YEAR

Stewart House

Canadian Cataloguing in Publication Data
Matthews, Caitlín, 1952–
    The Arthurian book of days

ISBN 0–7710–5858–6

1.   Arthurian romances.   2.   Literary calendars
I.   Matthews, John, 1948–   .   II.   Title.

PN6071.A84M38 1990   808.8'0351   090–093632–0

Published in Canada in 1990 by
Stewart House
481 University Avenue
Toronto, Ontario M5G 2E9

An Eddison · Sadd Edition
Edited, designed and produced by
Eddison Sadd Editions Limited
St Chad's Court, 146B King's Cross Road,
London WC1X 9DH

Phototypeset by Bookworm Typesetting, Manchester
Origination by Columbia Offset, Singapore
Printed and bound produced by Mandarin Offset, Hong Kong

CONTENTS

INTRODUCTION

The legends of King Arthur and his Knights of the Round Table remain evergreen in our imagination. But how did these stories begin? Legend and history have overlapped to such an extent that it is very difficult to establish the truth behind them. Yet before the Arthur of legend was the Arthur of history: the battle-lord, Artos, who defended Britain in the century after the departure of the Roman legions. Evidence for his life is scanty, but archaeologists and historians attest to the existence of a war-leader who lived about the beginning of the sixth century: a man who became a legend because of his ability to weld together the scattered confederacy of British tribes against the incursions of the invading Saxons. Here was the first appearance of the Pendragon, who was to become known as King Arthur. About him gathered tribal lords and kinsmen in whose names we see the faint traces of later knightly heroes: Gwalchmai (Gawain), Cei (Kay), Bedwyr (Bedivere) and Owain. The earliest British manuscripts, the *Welsh Triads*, themselves speak of great men and women of antiquity, of Arthur's companions, and name his wife, Gwenhwyfar (Guinevere), the most beautiful woman of the kingdom.

Artos the battle-lord lived on in the tales of the Cymry – the native British Celts – long after the Saxons established their kingdoms; for them, he lived beyond the sunset, ready to appear at his country's need. Nor did his story fade as the Celts withdrew westwards and northwards. In 1136 Geoffrey of Monmouth wrote his mythic *History of the Kings of Britain*, drawing on these ancient stories, but transforming them into medieval tales of a great Christian king with a court of paladins or knights. Since then Geoffrey's book has been a major source for Arthur's life and deeds, which have been added to, changed and adapted by each successive generation of writers.

To the elegant courts of twelfth-century Europe came such story-tellers as Chrétien de Troyes, Robert de Boron, Hartmann von Aue, Wolfram von Eschenbach and Eliert von Auberge, each of whom brought their own personal vision to the Matter of Britain, as the legends of King Arthur became known. Anonymous authors added such exciting adventures as *Sir Gawain and the Green Knight*, the *High History of the Holy Grail*, and *The Story of Merlin*. One of the first books to be printed on William Caxton's press was Sir Thomas Malory's *Le Morte DArthur*, in which many of the earliest stories were retold for a new and wider audience.

And so the battle-leader of history became the royal Arthur: Imperial ruler, chivalry's pattern, defender of the weak, giver of justice. His leather battle-harness was exchanged for plate armour, his cavalry *spatha* (sword) for a two-handed broadsword. Thus re-armed, Arthur lived on to fight new battles, now against dragons, giants and sorceresses. Always his companions, his wife and queen, Guinevere; his knights, Lancelot, Gawain, Gareth; his counsel-

lors, Merlin and the Lady of the Lake; his arch-enemies, Morgain le Fay, Morgause and Mordred, went with him.

Since the first wandering poets spread the stories of Arthur throughout the civilized world there has been a continuing interest in the Matter of Britain. In more recent times the Arthurian legends have been presented afresh by poets such as Alfred Lord Tennyson and Charles Williams, by novelists such as T.H. White, Rosemary Sutcliff, John Steinbeck, Mary Stewart and Marion Zimmer Bradley. To these printed works may be added such films as *Camelot* and *Excalibur*.

King Arthur is not the property of Britain: from Ireland to Russia, from Iceland to Italy, his tale is told and retold. It seems that every country finds a universal constant in the Arthurian legends. France has its legends of Charlemagne and his Peers, Russia its Knights of the Golden Table, Germany its Teutonic Knights – each reflecting in its own way the chivalric code established by Arthur and his knights. Monarchs have traced their descent from him, while the oppressed have looked to the King who will come again to rescue them from unjust rulers.

The stories which make up this particular book are drawn from many sources and many countries. Many are given here in English-language versions for the first time. In selecting from the almost endless variety of Arthurian literature we have followed certain guidelines. The stories must contribute something to the overall pattern of the mythic cycle which underlies all Arthurian works. They must be where possible fresh and unusual and convey the spirit of the originals. To this end also we have used a language which allows the rhythms of speech and of epic literature to convey the power of the stories. The compression necessary to encompass 365 stories (actually 366), without making the book unwieldy, has not always been easy, and we are aware that some details have been lost. However, we are satisfied that we have not done ill by the spirit of the originals, and hope that the final effect is one of excitement and wonder.

The book is intended primarily to be used in the same way that the original Books of Days were used in the Middle Ages – as a series of texts for every day of the year. Read in this way, and with the accompanying pictures – many of which are linked to the stories for the first time since they appeared in the Middle Ages – the book allows the reader to follow the stories around the wheel of the year, not just once but as often as he or she pleases. New facets of the stories, details missed the first time round, will thus become clearer with each successive reading.

While we have remained faithful to the texts in most instances, we have not hesitated, where this seemed necessary, to supply missing parts of the story, or linking passages between one and another. The very nature of the book requires that we break up the stories into pieces and this has occasionally led to extreme compression and even, in a couple of instances, to combining two separate stories in one. Finally, a short bibliography will be found at the end of the book. This is intended as both a source of further reading for those who wish to read the stories in full, and as an indication of the wide-ranging sources we have used to compile this collection.

John and Caitlín Matthews
London, 1989

HOW TO USE
THIS BOOK

The Arthurian Book of Days is arranged so that each day commemorates an event in the Arthurian cycle. The narrative of Arthur's life is not told straightforwardly from January to December but, as with anyone's life, events occur on certain days in different years. The Chronicle is included so that the reader can also follow the stories of the cycle consecutively.

The authors have determined these commemorations from their examination of a full range of texts, so that we can say with certainty that, for instance, the entry of the Green Knight happens at Christmas or that the Grail appears at Pentecost. However, some events are not associated with particular dates; for these, we have chosen special days with an eye sensitive to the general chronology of events and to the nature of the material.

Certain patterns and shapings are particular to the story cycle and these give us our Arthurian year. Rather like the Christian year and the Calendar of Saints, with which the characters of the Arthurian and medieval worlds would have been very familiar, there is a certain arbitrary determination of commemorations.

The reader may thus choose to read the book in one of three ways: first, as it is set forth in its seasonal unfolding from January to December; secondly, by following up particular stories or incidents which do not necessarily follow the chronological order of the cycle. (Within the text, dates will be found at the end of some stories which link them forward to the next, as in the 1st January story: ▷ 17th July indicates the continuation. Where the stories follow date-order in a natural sequence a simple ▷ sign will be found.) The third method is to use the Chronicle (pages 186–90) as a guide to the whole Arthurian cycle.

Note: some of the illustrations are curved, because the manuscripts could not always be dismantled for photography.

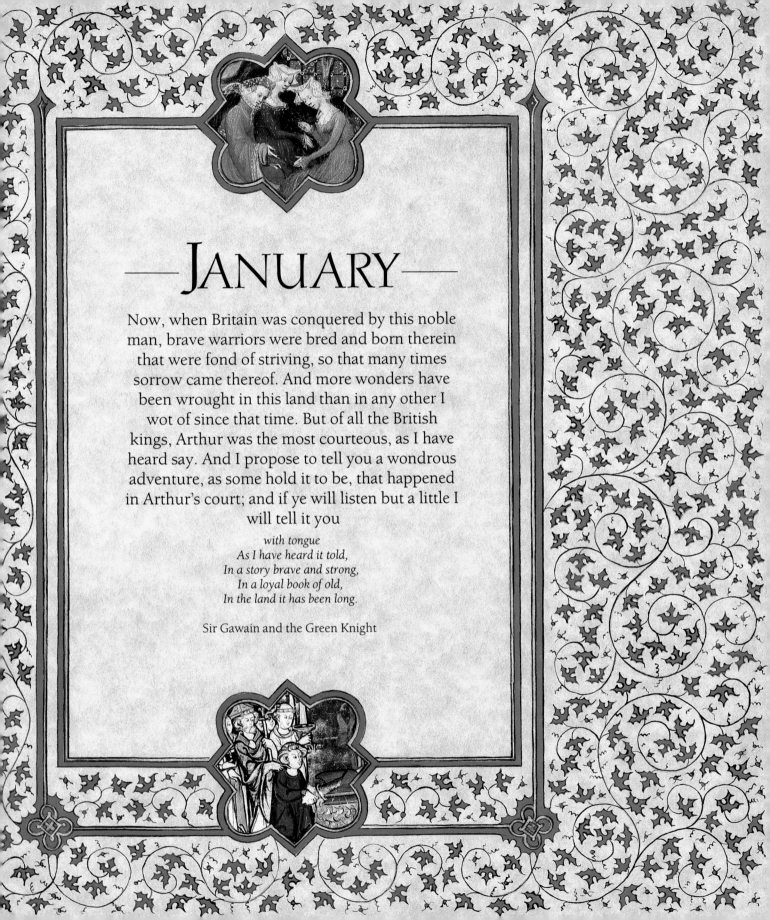

January

Now, when Britain was conquered by this noble
man, brave warriors were bred and born therein
that were fond of striving, so that many times
sorrow came thereof. And more wonders have
been wrought in this land than in any other I
wot of since that time. But of all the British
kings, Arthur was the most courteous, as I have
heard say. And I propose to tell you a wondrous
adventure, as some hold it to be, that happened
in Arthur's court; and if ye will listen but a little I
will tell it you

with tongue
As I have heard it told,
In a story brave and strong,
In a loyal book of old,
In the land it has been long.

Sir Gawain and the Green Knight

In the top part of the picture, the young Arthur draws the
Sword from the Stone in Westminster Abbey while clerics and
knights look on. In the bottom part he lays the sword on the
altar in preparation for making his knightly and kingly vows.

1ˢᵗ January

A great company met in the city of London on a bright day at the beginning of the year. Kings and knights from every part of the land came to try the great test of the Sword. Among them came Sir Ector of the Forest Sauvage and his son and foster-son, Kay and Arthur. Kay was to receive knighthood that day and to fight for the first time in the grand tournament. But when it was almost time for the mêlée Kay noticed that he had left his sword behind. He commanded Arthur, who was acting as his squire, to fetch it, but when the boy arrived back he found their lodgings locked up. Desperate, he ranged through the streets in search of a weapon, and came upon a quiet and deserted place where he saw a sword sticking up out of an anvil and a stone. Unthinkingly he snatched out the sword, and at once felt dizzy as what seemed to be great voices roared and shouted in his head. Throwing off this, he hastened to where Kay waited and gave the sword into Kay's hands. Staring, Kay studied it, recognizing the sword from the stone. He turned at once to Sir Ector and said: 'Father. This is the Sword. I am the new King.' But Ector looked long at him and said only: 'Show me.' And of course Kay could not, for though he replaced the Sword he could not draw it forth again. Arthur alone was able to do that, though others tried, even to the number of a thousand, before they would believe. Then voices roared about him in truth, and they were crying: 'Long live King Arthur'. But he never forgot his foster-parents, and at Ector's request he forgave Kay his momentary lapse and made him Seneschal of all Britain, which office he served faithfully, despite his sharp tongue and impatient ways.   ▷ 17ᵀᴴ July

▷ 17ᵀᴴ July

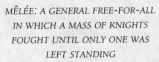

MÊLÉE: A GENERAL FREE-FOR-ALL IN WHICH A MASS OF KNIGHTS FOUGHT UNTIL ONLY ONE WAS LEFT STANDING

2ⁿᵈ January

In the Queen's garden at Camelot Lancelot sat at ease, until one of Guinevere's ladies began to tease him about his skills as a hunter. 'I know of a deer that none may catch,' she said, 'A deer with one white foot. Not even you, Sir Lancelot, could capture her.' And Lancelot, who was not used to being made sport of in this way, took her words to heart. That very day he set out in search of the white-footed hart: he rode all day and all night, sometimes resting, until he came to a part of the forest that he did not recognize. At the top of a steep hill he found a cave, and there an ancient hermit sat, taking the sun. 'Greeting, holy father,' said Lancelot, 'Do you know aught of a white-foot deer?' The hermit looked at him with faded eyes and said: 'I have seen her often. Every morning she comes this way.' Lancelot slept that night in the hermit's cave. Next morning he kept watch, and there, sure enough, came the white-foot hart – but not alone. She came with a lion and a leopard, and with other beasts Lancelot did not recognize. 'Now I think I have been sent on a strange errand,' said the knight, and set out to stalk the deer. But when he caught her it was no deer at all, but the very same maiden who had provoked him in the Queen's garden. She would have had sport with him then, but Lancelot sternly denied her, and with a laugh she was gone, none knew where. Nor was she ever seen at the court again, but Lancelot, dreaming that night, saw her in the castle of his foster-mother the Lady of the Lake, and smiled to know that he was still cared for.

3rd January

When the Round Table had been established for almost ten years, King Arthur found himself in conflict with the young lord of Surluse, a hotheaded youth named Galehaut the Haut Prince. The trouble began when the Prince claimed certain lands belonging to Arthur. A small force was sent to persuade him of his mistake; it returned, somewhat bloodied, bearing the Prince's arrogant denial of Arthur's right. Next to go was Lancelot, with a dozen Round Table knights and a hundred soldiers. They met the forces of Galehaut in a brief but furious battle. During this Lancelot unhorsed the Prince, and instead of killing him, helped him back into the saddle. Galehaut was so impressed by this chivalrous act that he called an end to the conflict and sued for peace. He then requested to be made a knight of the Round Table at Lancelot's hands and no other. They journeyed to Camelot together and Arthur magnanimously granted his wish. From this time Galehaut became Lancelot's most staunch friend, offering him gifts and even castles, all of which he courteously declined. Galehaut, however, never ceased to look for ways to please his hero, ever showing him gratitude and affection. ▷

4th January

As a result of the peace which now existed between the realms of Surluse and Britain, Arthur and Guinevere travelled to visit Galehaut the Haut Prince. He made them royally welcome in his greatest castle, and was especially glad to see Lancelot. He had not taken long to see how things lay with Lancelot and the Queen, and he saw a means to repay the great knight for his chivalry in the recent war. He had a private garden in his castle, with a secret gate kept always locked. Here he liked to sit and dream of adventure and conquest. Now he contrived to ask both Lancelot and the Queen to join him, and there, it is said, the lovers exchanged first words and finally a kiss – sealing their passion forever in that moment. But perhaps from guilt at the knowledge now possessed by his friend, Lancelot avoided Galehaut for a time, and shortly afterwards departed on a long quest in which he was, for a time, believed lost. ▷

In the garden of Galehaut's castle, Lancelot and
Guinevere exchange their first kiss, watched over by
the Haut Prince himself. In the background,
Guinevere's ladies are busy with their sewing.

13

The Green Knight holds aloft his severed head and commands Gawain to seek him out for a return blow a year from that day. Arthur, Guinevere and two knights watch in horror.

5th January

Galehaut searched long and hard for his friend, until he began to suffer a wasting sickness. He retired to his castle and, a few weeks later, died. Lancelot, returned at last from his arduous quest, heard the news with sorrow. With bowed head he went to pray at the grave of the young man who had so briefly graced this life.

6th January

The Christmas court at Camelot was always attended by all able-bodied members of the Round Table Fellowship. One year, as the company were awaiting the procession of supper, into the hall rode the most terrifying figure ever to be seen in that place of marvels. Gigantic in stature, he had green hair and green skin, and eyes as red as blood. He was dressed in green from top to toe and rode a horse of the same colour. In one hand he carried a great axe and in the other a bough of holly. Reining in before Arthur, he surveyed the stunned court with an arrogant stare. Then, in a great voice, he bellowed: 'Who rules here?' 'I am Arthur,' said the King quietly. 'I am the master of this place.' 'Then,' boomed the giant, 'I propose a Christmas game – open to any man here with the courage to play. Any one who chooses may deliver a blow with this axe of mine . . . on condition that he then take a return blow from me.'

Silence followed this speech, and none moved to take up the 'game'. Rolling his red eyes, the Green Knight stared about the court, challenging each and every knight for a response. Then, as Arthur himself, angry at the slowness of his knights, half rose in his seat, the young Gawain stepped forward. 'I claim this right,' he said, and took the Green Knight's proffered axe. Then, as the giant bent his knee and lowered his head to expose his neck, Gawain hefted the great blade and brought it down, shearing through flesh and bone, severing the green head, and biting into the tiled floor.

The green head fell, rolled, was kicked from foot to foot. Then the body moved, striding, uncertain, steadied, bent and picked up the head by its hair. The red eyes rolled, the green lips parted, and the words came forth: 'In a year, Sir Gawain, at the Green Chapel, there to take your blow.' Then the monstrous knight, turning disdainfully on his heel, set his head upon green shoulders and mounting, rode from the hall, leaving men shaken and uncertain, women weeping and distraught.

Arthur, finding strength in the moment, called out: 'Let the feast begin. We have seen our Christmas wonder. Let us celebrate the birth of our Saviour with good cheer.' But to Gawain he said, aside, 'Courage, nephew, the light still rules at Camelot. We shall illumine the dark.'

▷ 21ST DECEMBER

7th January

Perceval had a sister called Dindrane. She had been raised by holy sisters in the seclusion of a forest and now she dwelt alone as an anchoress. One day the old hermit who was her confessor came and told her that the evil Lord of Castle Mortal was wreaking devastation on all the country round and that it had come to him in a dream that this wicked knight might be overcome by a piece of the Holy Shroud of Our Lord. But this precious relic dwelt in the Perilous Cemetery, a place of such ill repute and dread that none, not even the most courageous, dared brave its horrors.

'Let me go there, good father,' cried Dindrane, 'For I would follow the way of spiritual chivalry, even as my brother learns the use of arms.' And the hermit, after pondering long and deeply and seeking guidance in prayer, permitted her to make a vigil there, and prayed long over her that she be not affrighted by the horrors of that place.   ▷

ANCHORESS: A FEMALE HERMIT

8th January

Around midnight, Dindrane entered the cemetery and commended her soul to God at the sight of flaming swords and the decayed forms of damned souls which haunted there. She came at last to a chapel wherein was a statue of Our Lady. Before the altar was the relic she sought. With great reverence she took the cloth to her bosom and there stowed it safely. As she did so an angelic voice spoke to her: 'Dindrane, be advised that the Holy Grail shall shortly appear in this land. Prepare yourself for this great quest, for you, of all women, are destined to see the glory of Our Saviour. Go now and take this cloth and deliver it to the holy hermit and then make your way to Lands Adventurous, there to seek your brother.' And Dindrane crossed herself devoutly and was glad that the way of spiritual chivalry should lead to such high purpose.

9th January

Arthur's court were impatiently waiting for their supper. No one could touch food before the King and he would only eat after a wonder had happened. It was with relief that they saw a maiden ride into court. 'You believe yourself to be honourable because of the deeds that are performed by the Round Table Fellowship, but I tell you that greater honour awaits all who come to Ireland and seek the marvels of Rigomer. My lady bids you find great wealth and favours.' They sat dumbfounded as the maiden rode out. Lancelot begged leave to pursue her and win honour on behalf of all who sat at the Round Table, and Arthur granted it.   ▷ 21ST FEBRUARY

MAGE: *magician; wise man*

Merlin tutors the young Arthur in the ways of the world, preparing him for the duties of kingship. Sir Ector, Arthur's foster-father, watches.

10th January

From Tintagel Merlin travelled deep into the Forest Sauvage. He came at last to the castle of Sir Ector, a brave old knight who had served Uther Pendragon well. This was the home Merlin had chosen for the young prince, though he spoke only of an orphaned child to Ector and his wife. They, awed by the presence of the Mage and feeling pity for the squalling brat in his arms, agreed to care for the child. And so Arthur, the son of Uther and Igrain, vanished from the sight of all men, and grew up amid the rides of the forest. He learned to fight and to hunt and hawk, and played rough-and-tumble games with Kay, Ector's true son, who became his brother in the carefree deeds of childhood, and whom he grew to love. Merlin came, whenever he could, and taught the boy other kinds of knowledge – of the stars and the power that moved them, and some little of the ways of the great world which he would one day enter.

▷ 31ST DECEMBER

11th January

Gorlois and Igrain of Cornwall had three daughters: Morgain, Morgause, and Elaine. After the death of their father, Uther Pendragon saw to their futures. Morgause and Elaine he allowed to remain with their mother until they reached marriageable age, but Morgain he sent to a Sisterhood of Nuns at the ancient abbey of Amesbury. There she learned quickly much more than the good women could teach her, after which she sought further afield in books not often read. And it is said that from this time she first turned to necromancy, becoming in time a great sorceress. But she never forgot the wrong done to her family by Uther, and this maybe fostered the animosity against her half-brother Arthur, which caused so much hurt to him in later years.

▷ 10TH JANUARY

12th January

In the times of King Arthur, the Empress of Rome dreamed of a great sow that was followed through the streets by a dozen smaller pigs. The Emperor announced that he would give a reward to whoever among his subjects could explain this riddle.

In another part of his kingdom lived a maiden named Grisandole, whose father had fallen into disgrace and had died, leaving his daughter without an inheritance. When she heard of the Empress's dream, and the great reward, Grisandole decided to try her luck. Dressing as a man and calling herself 'Avenable', she travelled to Rome, and there heard how a stag had appeared which, turning into an ancient wildman, had claimed to be able to answer the riddle, but had vanished before giving it. Now everyone was searching for him. Grisandole decided to search also, and went into the great forest to the north of the city. ▷

Merlin appears at the court of the Roman Emperor in the shape of a stag. Shortly afterwards he disappears into the woodlands and is hunted by the disguised maiden Grisandole.

13th January

Grisandole found him almost immediately, and brought him back to Rome, where the Emperor questioned him. And the old man laughed and said: 'The Empress's dream is easily explained. She is even now entertaining twelve "maidens", who are really youths in disguise. Thus she herself is the great sow and they the pursuing pigs.'

And so it proved to be. The Empress and her lovers were executed forthwith, while 'Avenable', restored to her real identity, was given back her father's lands and much praised for her courage and spirit. As for the old wildman, he was none other than Merlin, travelling about the world as was his wont, in search of knowledge and wrongs to set right.

14th January

Perceval was a young man who had never known the love of woman. He was already recognized as one of Arthur's greatest knights but he was not one to bide at court, for he had been raised in the woods. Once, when he was abroad, he chanced upon a glade wherein snow lay fair and white. A hawk had killed a duck, and now the body of the fowl lay tumbled in the snow and a raven feasted upon it. The blackness of the raven, the redness of the blood and the whiteness of the snow brought to Perceval's mind a vision that haunted him – of a woman whose image he had known since he became a man, whom he had never seen and perhaps would never meet. And she spoke to his heart: 'Perceval, there lies before you a great quest. Will you undertake to seek the Grail and heal the Wasteland, for though you see me beautiful now, soon I shall know the sorrow of devastation?'

▷

15th January

Perceval remained a long time, transfixed by the blood in the snow. And so he would have stayed, communing with the spirit of the earth itself, had it not been for Kay and Gawain riding by. 'The loon has fallen into a trance,' laughed Kay, and buffeted Perceval across the shoulder with a good-humoured slap. Perceval absently brushed Kay with the butt of his spear and broke Kay's collar-bone. Gawain approached more carefully and studied the young knight. At length, he spoke gently: 'Are you thinking upon the lady of your heart?' And Perceval, who would never know a woman, sighed and breathed, 'I have looked upon her who is my eternal love. The world is changed for me for ever.' And Gawain, accompanied by the moaning Kay, rode back to court with the young knight, who ever afterwards communed with the lady who was the land's life.

▷ 20TH JULY

16th January

Perceval wandered for a whole year in remorse, seeking to make himself better by valorous deeds. Each night, he dreamed of a marvellous island on which thirty-three wondrous men, sage as elders, sat down to eat; the floor of the hall where they were opened so that Perceval could hear the very voice of the earth and all that had ever lived thereon mourning and lamenting. And it put him in mind of the people of the past, those who were imprisoned in Hell, and of the descent of Our Lord there to rescue those in captivity and give them hope of Heaven. Then for pity he awoke weeping, and resolved to seek thereafter for the Castle of Ageless Elders.

17th January

It was seldom that Arthur went forth adventuring, but one day he rode out incognito. He triumphed in a tournament against a fierce knight named the Merciless Lion. The prize for winning the tournament, as had been prophesied by Merlin long since, was a parrot which acclaimed Arthur as the best knight in the world. ▷

18th January

When asked by what name he would be known, Arthur replied: 'The Knight of the Parrot', and he went on to overcome many dangers. He rescued the Lady Blonde Hair from the depredations of the Fish Knight, a fearsome monster whose body, arms and armour were all one living being. ▷

19th January

Arthur encountered a giant, against whom he fought till the hour of nones. As it grew dark, he was able to strike a lucky blow at the giant's leg which severed it. As the giant lay dying, he imparted three noble precepts which his father had taught him: to recognize one's saviour, to realize the good and evil which one may do with one's hands and mouth, and, lastly, to know oneself. Arthur upheld these truths his whole life through. ▷ 17TH DECEMBER

NONES: 3.00 PM

20th January

A great feast was to be held at Caerleon, and to it came all the greatest of Arthur's knights and lords. When the meal was about to begin, a fair-faced youth entered with a gift for the King from a lord named Margon – a magnificent ivory horn with three bands of gold around it. Arthur received it gladly and offered food and a place at table to the youth. But he demurred, saying that a mere squire should not sit at table with such great knights, and departed hastily.

When he was gone Arthur looked again at the horn and saw that there were letters written around it, which read: WHOSO DRINKETH OF THIS HORN, THOUGH HIS LADY HATH HAD BUT A SINGLE DISLOYAL THOUGHT, IT SHALL SPILL WINE UPON HIM. Then Arthur called at once for wine and drank, but as he did so a stream of wine spilled out of the horn onto his robe. In silence he stared at Guinevere, who sat, blushing rose-red. 'My lord,' said she, 'I have ever been good and faithful to thee, but I did once give a ring of mine to a young knight to encourage him to remain here at your court. This was out of love for you and no other.' And Gawain spoke up also: 'My lord, who can claim that his wife or lady never thought to do some

deed she might regret. Let every man here try the horn – I will gladly begin.' And Arthur gave him the horn, which spilled quantities of wine upon Gawain, who laughed aloud and gave it to Kay, to whom the same occurred. Arthur began to smile himself now, and soon all the court was in uproar – though, it must be said, not all the women joined in the laughter. But since all were seen to fail, none could think themselves better or worse than the rest.

OGAM: THE ANCIENT SECRET LANGUAGE OF POETS

— 21st January —

*B*ound to King Mark's court by the presence of Isolt, Tristan sought ever new ways to meet her in secret. He even devised a way of sending messages to her by floating pieces of bark on which were carved signs in Ogam. Once, becoming suspicious, Mark hid in the branches of a tree where he knew the lovers met. But Tristan espied him reflected in the stream which ran beneath the tree, and was able to divert suspicion by acting coolly towards Isolt.   ▷ 30TH JUNE

— 22nd January —

*O*f all the places in the wide woodlands through which the Fellowship of the Round Table went on adventure, none had a more terrible reputation than the Chapel Perilous. Many had attempted its trials and few had escaped whole. There in time came Sir Lancelot, and he saw that before the Chapel were many shields that he knew, hung upon a tree, but all upside-down. And before the entrance to the Chapel was a graveyard, in which were twenty knights all armed in black, and as they saw him they drew their swords and within their helmets he saw faces of bone that grinned and gnashed at him horribly. But still Lancelot came on undaunted, and fought his way through the spectres into the Chapel itself. There he saw the body of a knight lying under a cloth with a great sword clasped in his hands. And Lancelot took the sword and with it cut away part of the cloth – though why, he scarcely knew. The earth itself seemed to move as he did so, and in fear he quit the place. Outside he met a damsel who stood before him and begged him to love her. 'For I made all this to test you,' she said, 'knowing that only Lancelot could achieve these tests.' Lancelot looked sternly at her and said, 'Madam, if you know who I am you must surely know also that I may love no woman save my lady the Queen.' 'Then I would rather you were dead and that I might have your body to hold!' cried the sorceress, and she summoned the black-clad knights, who rose and attacked Lancelot again. A hard time he had of it, but in the end he laid them all low, and rode away. And it is said that the sorceress, who was named Hellwas, afterwards died of grief and came to haunt the Chapel Perilous.   ▷

23rd January

As Lancelot rode on his way, slowly, for he had sustained many wounds in his battle with the black knights, he met a damsel he knew, the sister of Sir Meliot de Logres, a brave knight of the Fellowship. When she saw him she clapped her hands for joy and begged him to come with her to a hermitage where poor Sir Meliot lay sick. 'For I have had a dream but last night,' she said, 'that you would come and would make him whole again with a piece of cloth which you carry.' At which Lancelot remembered the piece he had taken from the Chapel Perilous, and rode on apace. When he reached the wounded knight he took forth the miraculous piece of cloth and laid it upon his hurts. They were immediately healed, and so he did likewise with his own hurts and they too were at once healed up. ▷

24th January

Lancelot heard about a castle called the Dolorous Gard, so named because no man who had attempted to conquer its evils had ever succeeded. So of course Lancelot turned for the place at once. When he arrived there he found a damsel waiting for him whom he recognized as being a servant of the Lady of the Lake, his foster-mother. She said: 'Sir Lancelot, beware. This is an evil place and will demand all the strength you possess.' 'I am ready,' said he. 'Then know that there are three gates to this castle which you must pass, and at each one you will find twenty, thirty and forty knights waiting. You must overcome them all before you enter, and there are other trials if you succeed.'

So Lancelot went forward and was met and challenged, just as the damsel had foretold. That day he did the greatest work that ever a knight of the Round Table did in one space of time. He overcame all ninety of the knights who guarded the gates to the castle, and though sorely wounded he was still able to walk through the innermost gate. There he met an aged man who showed him wordlessly to a graveyard within the castle. There were many tombs of knights of the Round Table that had been slain there. And in the centre was a great slab of metal on which was written: ONLY HE WHO CONQUERS THIS PLACE SHALL LIFT THIS SLAB, AND HIS NAME IS WRITTEN BENEATH. So Lancelot bent and with all his might lifted the slab until it stood upon one end. Beneath it was written in letters of untarnished gold, LANCELOT DU LAC.

Then he heard a great crashing noise and a huge knight attacked him, but Lancelot coolly slew him and thus ended the evil of the place, whose people came out to greet him and offer homage. He set free all the knights who were imprisoned there, including many of Arthur's men, and took the castle for his own. But the name he changed from 'Dolorous' to 'Joyous' Gard.

25th January

It had taken Perceval the whole of Twelfth Night to retrieve the chessboard he had so thoughtlessly pitched into the lake. This task done, he was now lodged at a mysterious castle where his host seemed to have a strange affliction. Being courteous, Perceval did not ask what ailed him. ▷

26th January

At dinner the next night, the lights dimmed and in came a mysterious procession which was accompanied by the most doleful weeping. A maiden bore a spear down which ran a great stream of blood. She was followed by damsels carrying candles of surpassing brightness. Last of all came the fairest maiden he had ever seen in his life, and what she bore in her hands made him want to sign himself devoutly. As the procession retreated, the question came to Perceval's lips: 'What does this signify?', but the words were never uttered. He looked upon his host's infirmities and forbore to question him. Strangely troubled, he went to his rest. ▷

At the Castle of the Grail, the innocent Perceval sees the Grail and the Wounded King but fails to ask the all-important question which will bring about healing.

Perceval sees the procession of the four Grail 'hallows' at the Castle of the wounded Fisher King.

27th January

Perceval awoke on the bank of a river. Gone was the castle, gone was everyone in it. As he sat amazed, the witch of Gloucester returned and berated him: 'You fool! You sat and watched the procession of the Grail itself and still you could not open your mouth. Because of you, there will be orphans and widows and men slain in battle! You will have to learn what misery really is! Know that your mother, whom you left, is long dead of grief at losing you. Come to your senses and be a man!' Perceval was grieved to hear her speak so. He fervently vowed that he would make pilgrimage to the ends of the earth to become a worthier knight.

THE WITCH OF GLOUCESTER:
PERCEVAL'S OTHERWORLDLY
TUTOR AT ARMS

28th January

When Arthur held court at Glastonbury, there came in a young man begging to be made a knight. As Arthur held the sword Excalibur to dub him, he asked the youth's name: 'My mother called me Libeaus Desconus.' And the court were much amused at this. Then King Arthur said, 'I dub you Sir Fair Unknown, in the name of St Mary and Her Fair Son.' And Fair Unknown was accorded the device of a griffin. ▷

29th January

The next day, when they sat down to eat, a maiden named Eleyne rode into the hall. 'My Lady of Sinadoun is being held captive in her own castle. Send one of your strongest men to release her!' And the knights of the court were loath to oblige, so imperiously did she make her demand. Then Fair Unknown sprang forward and begged this quest. 'I give you this young knight to aid you. May his youthful deeds liberate your lady.' Eleyne was dismayed to be fobbed off with such a youth and complained about his inexperience as they rode off together in search of her lady. ▷ 3RD OCTOBER

30th January

Arthur came upon Guinevere weeping and asked her why: 'Because the fame of the Round Table is becoming stale. I had a dream that you should go to the Chapel of St Austin and pray that God strengthen you again with great deeds.' And Arthur knew that Guinevere wept still for Loholt and for the failure of their line, for only Mordred remained to succeed him, and that young man was but a shadow of gentle Loholt. 'I shall go tomorrow with my squire Cahus,' and he called the boy to make all ready. ▷

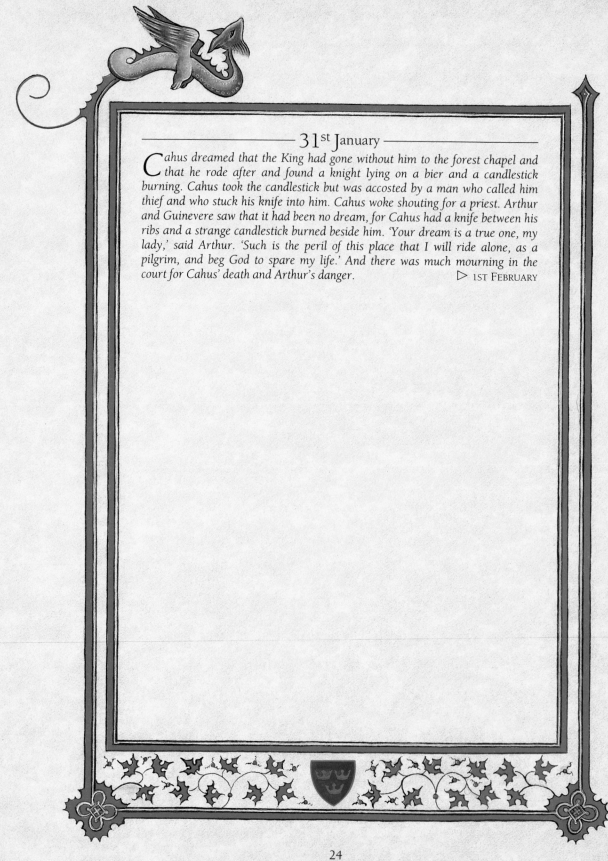

31st January

Cahus dreamed that the King had gone without him to the forest chapel and that he rode after and found a knight lying on a bier and a candlestick burning. Cahus took the candlestick but was accosted by a man who called him thief and who stuck his knife into him. Cahus woke shouting for a priest. Arthur and Guinevere saw that it had been no dream, for Cahus had a knife between his ribs and a strange candlestick burned beside him. 'Your dream is a true one, my lady,' said Arthur. 'Such is the peril of this place that I will ride alone, as a pilgrim, and beg God to spare my life.' And there was much mourning in the court for Cahus' death and Arthur's danger.

▷ 1ST FEBRUARY

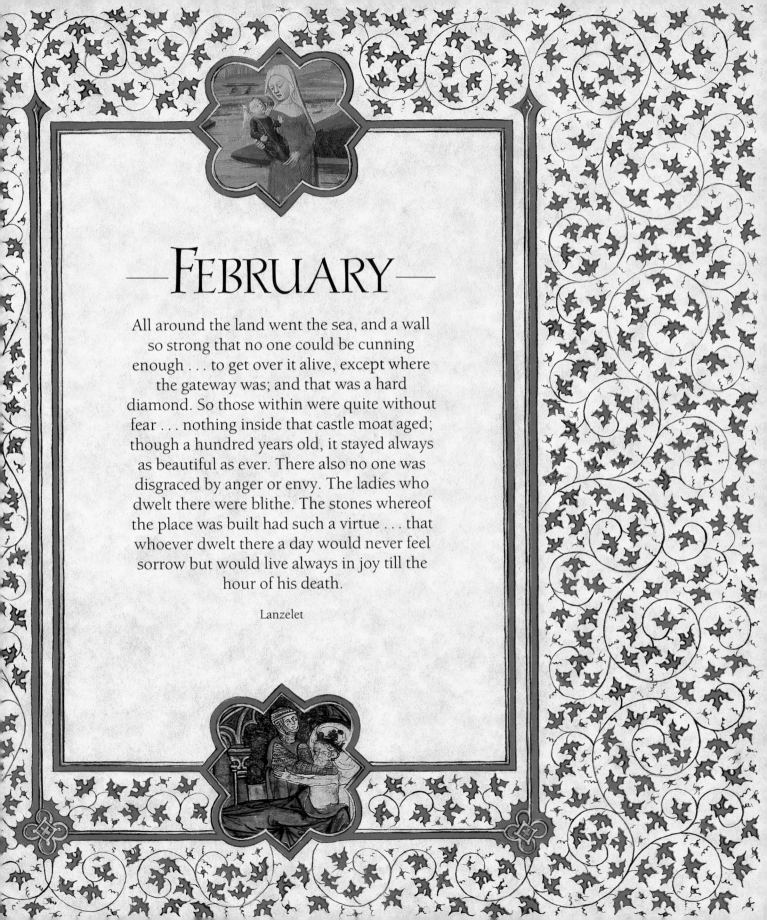

February

All around the land went the sea, and a wall
so strong that no one could be cunning
enough . . . to get over it alive, except where
the gateway was; and that was a hard
diamond. So those within were quite without
fear . . . nothing inside that castle moat aged;
though a hundred years old, it stayed always
as beautiful as ever. There also no one was
disgraced by anger or envy. The ladies who
dwelt there were blithe. The stones whereof
the place was built had such a virtue . . . that
whoever dwelt there a day would never feel
sorrow but would live always in joy till the
hour of his death.

Lanzelet

1st February

Arthur came to the Chapel of St Austin upon the eve of Candlemas and there he saw a hermit about to say Mass. Arthur remained at the door and watched all that took place. And he saw that beside the altar was a fair woman with a child in her lap. At the offertory, she gave her son into the hands of the priest, who raised the child instead of the sacramental wafer. Arthur hid his eyes from this awesome sight. And when he looked again he saw that the hermit held a bleeding man upon the altar for a brief time. Then the bleeding figure became a child again and the woman received him back into her arms and said: 'Sire, you are my father, and my son, and my lord and my guardian,' to which Arthur added reverently, 'And the guardian of everyone.' The hermit came out to where Arthur was and bade him reform his life, for a great wonder would soon enter it and he should be prepared. This Arthur promised to do, and he spent the night in prayer and vigil. ▷

2nd February

As Arthur left the chapel in the morning, he came upon a damsel being carried off against her will. Though he was fatigued from his vigil, he slew the knight and set the damsel at liberty. In gratitude she cried, 'My thanks, sir knight. Tell me, by what name should I know you, so that I may tell everyone of your courage?' And Arthur modestly answered, 'I am Sir Arthur.' The damsel frowned. 'Of all names you could have borne, that is the worst. Everyone says that Arthur's court is the most ignoble in the land, that the King stays home to guard the Queen from abduction and that his knights follow his example in sloth and idleness.' And Arthur set her on her way and went dolefully home, having heard all he needed about himself.

SAMITE: A KIND OF RICH SILK

3rd February

Hard upon the Quest for the Grail, Sir Gawain stayed near a ruined chapel one night. And there he either dreamed, or thought he dreamed, that he saw a hand and arm enter through the door, and the arm was dressed in scarlet samite and the hand held a candle, while from it dangled a plain bridle. Gawain could make nothing of what had occurred. But in the morning there came a hermit who told him that these things betokened the reasons why he would never attain the Grail: for the hand spelled charity, the giving of wealth to the poor, the candle was faith, which in Gawain's case was far from steady, and the bridle stood for the governing of passion, which he could never attain to. Unabashed by this Gawain continued on his way.

4th February

Perceval rode for a long time seeking the court of King Arthur. He came upon a tent and, thinking it was a church, knelt and said his prayers. Then he entered and, seeing food set ready, fell upon it, famished. When he was sated he looked about him and saw a precious stone set in a ring. But the ring was on a hand and the hand belonged to a sleeping lady. Perceval remembered his mother's advice and drew off the ring; this awoke the lady, whom he then kissed. Not understanding her protests, Perceval, much refreshed, rode on in search of King Arthur. The lady's cries soon brought her lord knight, who roundly accused the pair of them of concupiscence, and her protestations of innocence were of no avail. So it was that Herzeloyde's advice brought her son into trouble. ▷

5th February

Perceval came at length to Arthur's court. As he entered the hall he saw a red knight insult the Queen and pour wine in her lap. Before any other could avenge Guinevere, Perceval followed the red knight and belaboured him so mightily with a wooden spear-shaft that he died. Perceval then tried to remove the knight's armour, but not knowing the way of things, ended by trying to cook the man in his armour, as though boiling a lobster. Owain saw his plight and helped him. 'For,' said he, 'You have earned this armour by your deeds. And if you stay with us, we will teach you knightly ways, and we will do well together.' So it was that the foolish woodland lad began to be shaped into the great Sir Perceval. ▷ 14TH JANUARY

6th February

When Lancelot and Gawain were riding near the seashore they encountered a knight named Moriaen, whose skin was black as night. They thought they had met the Foul Fiend himself, but Moriaen allayed their fears by his courteous speech. His father had been Sir Aglovale and he had begotten Moriaen upon a Moorish princess. Now his mother sent him to find his father. When Lancelot and Gawain heard that they offered him every assistance. ▷

7th February

It was as well that Lancelot and Gawain accompanied Moriaen on his quest for Aglovale, for every boatman, ostler and scullion ran from the sight of the handsome black knight. At last they discovered the place of Aglovale's retreat. There Moriaen begged his father to return to his mother and fulfil his promise to

At the Chapel of the Grail Arthur has a vision of the Blessed Virgin Mary, and thereafter carries her image always on his banner.

wed her. Then Aglovale remembered that he had plighted his troth to that lady long ago and had dishonoured her, and so he returned and became king of her country. Thereafter Moriaen often visited Logres and shared the tasks of the Round Table Fellowship.

8th February

King Mark of Cornwall had a brother named Boudwin, who was as popular as Mark was unpopular. For this reason Mark hated him, and when Boudwin overcame a fleet of Saracen pirates, thus earning the gratitude of Arthur himself, Mark's anger increased. He summoned Boudwin, his wife and their young son to visit him. After they had dined Mark picked a quarrel and then in a fit of rage stabbed his brother to the heart before his wife's eyes. She, terrified both for herself and her son, fled into the forest. Mark, beside himself, ordered a knight named Sir Sadok to pursue her and to make certain she never reached home. But Sadok was a worthy man, and when he overtook the lady, he warned her not to return home but to take refuge with her cousin in the castle of Arundel. This she did, while Sadok returned to King Mark and told him they were both dead. ▷ 14TH FEBRUARY

9th February

King Ban of Benoic was assailed by enemies and had to flee with his wife Clarine. They turned to see their castle in flames, and Clarine realized that her husband was mortally wounded. Carrying their baby boy on her shoulder, she helped Ban to a spring where he drank a draught. But she saw that he was too weak to rise, and in a while he gave up the ghost. In an excess of grief and fear, Clarine climbed a tree and fell into a deep sleep while she hid from the enemy. As she sheltered there, the Lady of the Lake came invisibly and stole away the child from her arms. But it was with foreknowledge that the faery woman did this, for Ban's enemies came upon the sleeping Queen and bore her away captive. They would surely have slain the little boy, had not the Lady of the Lake taken him safely to her island fastness. ▷ 13TH FEBRUARY

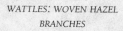

WATTLES: WOVEN HAZEL
BRANCHES

10th February

There lived in a far-off land a good and true knight named Titurel. One day, when he was nearing his fiftieth year, an angel appeared to him and told him that he had been chosen to serve the Fellowship of the Holy Grail. 'For at this time,' said the angel, 'the Grail rests in a church of wattles built by Joseph the

After the death of King Ban of Benoic and the
overrunning of his kingdom by an aggressive
neighbour, the Lady of the Lake carries the infant
Lancelot into her magical underwater kingdom.

Arimathean many years since in the land of Britain. You must seek now Muntsalvach, the Mountain of Salvation, where your steps will be guided, and there build for the Grail a fitting place.' ▷

11th February

Next day Titurel set forth on his journey, and just as the angel had promised his steps were led through the great forest to the foot of Muntsalvach. And there he found other men and women who had been called from the four corners of the land, and together they set about building a Temple of the Grail. That very night they climbed the mountain, and began levelling the surface on which to build. And when that was done, Titurel dreamed again, being told to go forth and look upon the mountain. There, engraved in lines of fire, was the ground-plan of the temple. Thereafter, in the long months that followed, the whole company were guarded and fed by no human agency, until the Temple was complete. ▷

12th February

When at last the Grail Temple stood firm, tower on shining tower, such as might be seen leagues distant, so the Holy Cup was installed in a jewelled reliquary at the heart of the building. And Titurel, inspired by God, spoke to those who had helped to build the place. 'Great deeds will be accomplished by those in search of that which we guard here. Let it be known that there shall be a new Knighthood, and a new Chivalry, in this place, and that we who are present shall found a Family of the Grail.' Thereafter, a new King ruled upon Muntsalvach, awaiting the time when seekers would come in quest of the Grail.

13th February

The Lady of the Lake lived upon a marvellous island where no one aged, where all was courtesy and delight. The island was inhabited by faery women and served by the mer-folk – sea people, half-fish, half-human. It was here that Clarine's son was raised. Mermen taught him the use of arms and how to hunt, but the boy grew in ignorance of how to ride a horse or what armour was, since all who lived there were of undying race and needed no defence from scathe. When the boy was nearly a man, he begged leave to know who he was, for he as yet had no name in that blessed place where every heart was known to other. The Lady of the Lake bade him go forth and overcome the best knight of the world and thus avenge her; for only so would he gain a name.

▷ 28TH NOVEMBER

14th February

*B*oudwin's lady lived on in hiding while her son, who was named Alisander le Orphelin, grew to manhood. Then, on the day he received knighthood, she gave him his father's bloody shirt and told him the story. He swore to avenge his father's death, but before that he took part in a tournament in which he won such renown that word of it reached Mark's ears. Then Mark was maddened, and chased through the halls of his castle in search of Sir Sadok. And, though that worthy knight escaped at this time, Mark had him pursued and slain secretly, and at the same time sent word to Morgain le Fay that a mighty knight who would aid Arthur against her was on his way to Camelot. ▷

15th February

*A*lisander le Orphelin was never to reach the place where the Fellowship of the Round Table met. On his way he had many adventures. A beautiful lady held him prisoner for a year, and after that he fell into the clutches of Morgain le Fay herself, who desired him greatly, both for his beauty and his strength. But Alisander met a lady named Alice le Belle Pilgrim, who upon seeing his face fell in love with him, and he with her. And by her wit she succeeded in freeing him from the stronghold of Morgain, and married him. But though she bore him a son, whom they named Bellengereus, their life together was to be brief. Mark's assassins finally caught up with Alisander and slew him. It was thus left to Bellengereus to avenge both his father and grandfather: this he did, in the end, after the breaking of the Fellowship, when he slew Mark in single combat.

16th February

*O*ne day, in excess of joy, Arthur kissed Guinevere in the sight of the court, which caused her great embarrassment. When she protested he said, 'But sweet, I know that your affection is known to me utterly.' 'You are mistaken, my lord,' said the Queen, 'in supposing that any man can know the nature or the heart of woman.' Then Arthur swore a great oath and, taking Kay and Gawain with him, he went on a quest to find out this very thing. ▷

17th February

*A*rthur met with many sage men, but none could tell him what he wished to know. He finally came to the house of Gorlagon, who bade him dismount and be comfortable, for he had a very long tale to tell concerning the nature and the heart of woman. 'Once there was a king whose fate was wound with that of a

sapling, planted at his birth. It was prophesied that the sapling could be made into a rod of shape-changing and so the king kept this secret safely for his own well-being. Now he married a woman who longed to know everything about him, for she wished to lie with her lover and be rid of the king. She plagued him day and night concerning the secret until the king told her all. She immediately prepared the sapling and tapped the king on the head and said, "Become a wolf and have the nature of a wolf but have the understanding of a man." The werewolf fled to another land and, in its rage and fury, wrought many terrible deeds, so that the lord of that place went out to hunt it.' Here Gorlagon broke off his tale and said, 'But I weary you, lords. Take your supper and we shall conclude our story later.' ▷

--------------------- 18th February ---------------------

Arthur, Kay and Gawain listened intently to the werewolf's adventures and calamities, never noticing the passing of time. Gorlagon told them of how the good lord had rescued the werewolf and brought it home, but that his lady feared it, for she was secretly in love with her steward and the werewolf had seen them together. She pretended that it had eaten her children and had attacked her, but the werewolf led the lord to where the children were safely locked up. Having caught his lady in a lie he had her burned and the steward flayed alive. 'Then the werewolf persuaded the lord to journey to his own land, by means of signs and mournful looks. Wherever they went, the lord heard complaints of the new king and how good their former king had been.' And here Gorlagon broke off. 'For now it is suppertime.' ▷

--------------------- 19th February ---------------------

Arthur begged Gorlagon to ignore the hour and to continue the story, and so they sat all night listening: 'The lord soon came to the perfidious queen's court. There he accused her and bade her fetch the shape-changing rod, and so the lord tapped the werewolf on the head and said, "Be a man and have the understanding of a man." And the werewolf resumed his former shape and divorced the queen and took a virtuous lady to wed … Now will you take supper?' asked Gorlagon. 'No,' said Arthur, 'not until you tell me who is that woman at your table who sits kissing that bloodstained head.' 'It is none other than the perfidious queen you heard me tell of. And the head is that of her lover. And I was once a werewolf, who am now a man. And I ask you, Arthur, of your great wisdom, what is the nature and the heart of woman?' And Arthur was too abashed to answer, but rode back to Camelot a sadder and wiser man.

20th February

*T*he ship which sailed from Britain, carrying Tristan in search of Mark's bride, made shore at last and he was perturbed to find that he recognized the place as being near the court of the Irish King. And it came to him that he knew the owner of the golden hair – Isolt herself, whom he loved and who loved him. But he was bound by his promise to his uncle to bring back the owner of the hair, and he went to the court, all openly, and announced himself by his own name. In this he took a risk, but he had become friendly with the king during his time there as Isolt's patient, and now he came as an emissary, offering peace between the two lands through the marriage of the king's daughter to his uncle the lord of Cornwall. As he made the offer, in his heart he longed to ask for Isolt for himself. But once the words were said they could not be taken back, and King Anguish was glad enough to end the bloodshed between the two lands. So it was that Tristan prepared to take ship once more for Cornwall, this time with Isolt at his side. ▷ 7TH MARCH

21st February

*L*ancelot sailed to Ireland in search of the marvels of Rigomer. Wherever he rode, good people warned him of going to that dread castle. As he drew nearer the place he met wounded knights, coming from their own encounter with its terrors. He also met many combative knights whom he overcame, and bade them sue Arthur for clemency. ▷ 24TH APRIL

22nd February

*I*n the days before the Pendragon family ruled Logres, Vortigern was King of Britain. Harried on all sides by Irish pirates, the Painted People of the north and the Saxons from the Eastern Seas, Vortigern invited the Saxon kings Horsa and Hengist to Logres and gave them grants of land in return for their help in repelling further invaders. ▷

23rd February

*T*he people of Britain were disquieted by their king's strategy, but they had sworn an oath by the sacred hallows of the land to uphold him. Some rebelled against the incursion of their land and there was open revolt and much slaughter. It was with misgiving that the nobility of Logres gathered at Caer Caradduc, where Vortigern had called a peace council. All attended in good faith, leaving their weapons without – all, that is, save Hengist's men, who secreted

long daggers in their boots. At the given signal of their lord, they drew these daggers and plunged them into the throats of their British companions. Following the terrible slaughter of this night, Vortigern fled to the mountains of Wales.

▷ 31ST JULY

----------- 24th February -----------

While Gawain was engaged on the Quest for the Grail he came to a fortress called the Castle of Enquiry, where he learned that his host's son had been taken away by an evil knight. He set out to rescue the youth and on the way came to a wondrous fountain covered by a pillared roof from which hung a vessel of gold. He was about to drink from this when a hermit appeared and told him it was not for him to do so. There came into sight three women garbed in white, one of whom carried some bread on a vessel of gold, the second wine in a vessel of ivory, and the third meat on a dish of silver. All were destined for King Pelles, who lay sick near at hand. Gawain remembered the Dolorous Blow of Balin and knew from this he must be close to the Grail, but he knew also that he must first discharge his duty to the lord of the Castle of Enquiry before going on.

▷ 6TH MARCH

----------- 25th February -----------

King Ambrosius of the Pendragon line was grieved at the slaughter of the Night of the Long Knives, when the flower of British nobility perished, and he resolved to build a worthy memorial for them. He summoned Merlin to contrive a lasting monument. Merlin directed him to bring certain medicinal and sacred stones from Ireland and erect them at Caer Caradduc, near Salisbury. Ambrosius' men were unable to move the stones without Merlin's help. With great solemnity, the stones were erected over the place where the great nobles of Britain lay interred. People thereafter called it Stonehenge.

----------- 26th February -----------

After many adventures, Gawain came to Rigomer, where the Britons were almost overcome by the terrible enchantments of that place. They had endured hot rain-showers, horned dogs and battling monks. Gawain, taking his courage in hand, crossed the bridge unarmed, as he had been instructed by his faery helper, Lorie. He quickly found the kitchens and discovered Lancelot in a sad condition, unknowing and uncaring of everything. Gawain noticed that all the prisoners wore rings upon their hands, and divined that this was the cause of

At the request of Aurelius Ambrosius, Merlin has erected Stonehenge as a memorial to those who were murdered by the Saxons in the Night of the Long Knives. Here he is shown with one of the giants traditionally supposed to have built the great circle.

their enchantment. He drew off first that which was on Lancelot's finger. It shattered into pieces on the floor and Lancelot knew his friend again and was ashamed of his wretched condition. Swiftly, Gawain removed the rings of the other imprisoned knights. ▷

27th February

Gawain then achieved the last two tests which would break the enchantments: he climbed the tower and gained the goshawk of Rigomer, and he struck the silver quintain. As he did so all the knights wounded by the enchantments of that place became healthy once more. Gawain then swore that, though he could not take the throne of Rigomer and marry the lady Dionise himself, he would find a worthy husband for her. Amid great rejoicing, Gawain and his companions bore Lancelot home.

28th February

Galahad, Perceval and Bors came to Corbin, the castle of the Wounded King. 'Greatly have I desired your coming,' cried King Pelles, 'For now my long pain shall have an ending.'

The three knights were led to a chapel wherein all the holy objects were housed: the spear which bled, the candles which burned and were not extinguished, and the vessel of the Grail itself. The chapel seemed full of a multitude of spirits, and when they saw that the priest was about to say Mass, using the holy objects, they knelt in prayer.

When the priest turned from the altar each knight saw a different thing, which was yet the same. Bors saw a handsome man vested like a priest. Perceval recognized the Head in the Dish, which he had seen before in his adventures. But Galahad looked up and hid his face, for he beheld the visage of the Saviour himself.

About that holy place was the beating of many wings, as of angels in a great throng. Each knight made his peace with God and came to receive the host. And as Galahad received into his hands the vessel of the Holy Blood, the one who stood in the place of the priest said: 'Do you know what it is that you hold, my son?' 'Tell me, lord,' said Galahad. 'This is the holy dish with which I celebrated my Last Supper on Sherthursday. And now you have seen what you most desired to see, though not as openly as I will yet show you. I bid you take this holy vessel to Sarras, the spiritual city, for it must pass out of Arthur's kingdom until a time appointed. Prepare yourself for that journey and take with you only Perceval and Bors.' ▷

◇

QUINTAIN: A TILTING-POST FOR KNIGHTS TO PRACTISE JOUSTING

◇

◇

SHERTHURSDAY: MAUNDY THURSDAY; THE DAY ON WHICH PEOPLE WERE SHAVEN OR SHRIVEN

◇

29th February

The next day Galahad took the Spear reverently in his hands, and approaching the King, touched the blade gently to the wounds in his thighs. And at once the wounds were healed. And at that same moment the wasteland was restored. Pelles rose to his feet with a cry of joy. 'Now may I rest at last!' he cried, and kneeling before the altar he gave up the ghost.

There was great rejoicing at the healing of the land, and solemn thanksgiving for the ending of King Pelles' pain. The three knights left the castle and returned to where the Ship of Solomon awaited them. And so they took ship for Sarras, bearing the Grail with them beyond the borders of Arthur's kingdom at last. To Perceval alone did Galahad impart his vision, and it seemed to him that his companion was like a man in a dream, albeit a holy one, and that he appeared more like an angel than a mortal man.

▷ 25TH MARCH

In the wondrous Castle of Corbin, Galahad, the chosen winner of the Grail, encounters the Grail King and is able, through the power of the Spear, to heal his terrible wounds.

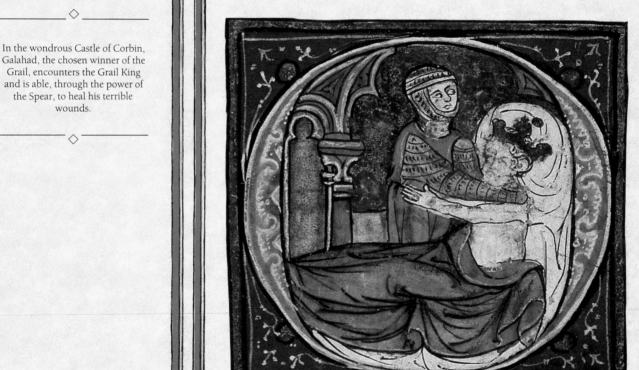

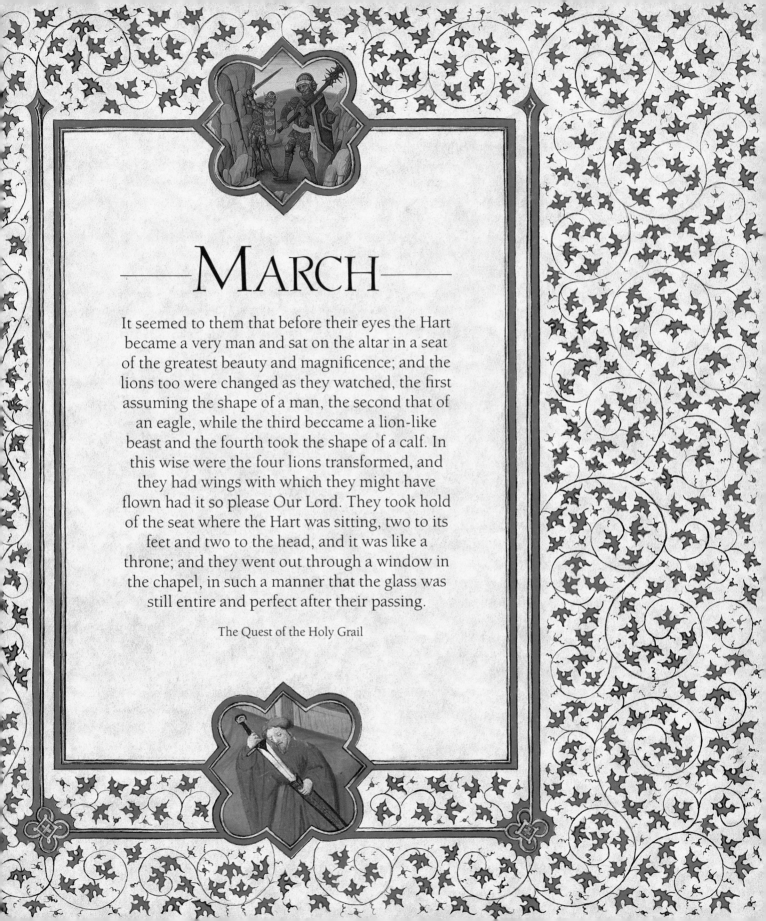

MARCH

It seemed to them that before their eyes the Hart
became a very man and sat on the altar in a seat
of the greatest beauty and magnificence; and the
lions too were changed as they watched, the first
assuming the shape of a man, the second that of
an eagle, while the third beccame a lion-like
beast and the fourth took the shape of a calf. In
this wise were the four lions transformed, and
they had wings with which they might have
flown had it so please Our Lord. They took hold
of the seat where the Hart was sitting, two to its
feet and two to the head, and it was like a
throne; and they went out through a window in
the chapel, in such a manner that the glass was
still entire and perfect after their passing.

The Quest of the Holy Grail

1st March

Lamorack de Galles was the eldest son of King Pellinore and one of the mightiest knights of the Round Table – second, some said, to Lancelot himself. But he had a guilty secret: he loved Queen Morgause of Orkney more than his life, for though the Queen was nearly fifty she still had the power to rouse men to passion. ▷

2nd March

One day, as she and Lamorack were abed together, and had fallen into a light sleep, Morgause's second son, Gaheries, came to her chamber. Seeing her there in the arms of her lover, hair spread across the pillows, a red anger came upon him. Drawing his sword he cut off his mother's head with a single blow. Then, filled with horror, he fled. Lamorack, waking at length, found himself in

Gaheries, second son of Morgause and Lot of Orkney, on discovering his mother abed with Lamorack de Galles, cuts off her head before fleeing, half-mad, into the forest.

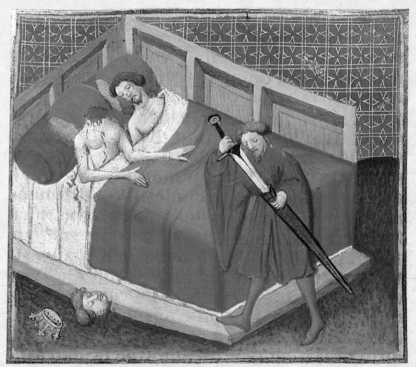

bed with a corpse. At the terrible sight he ran shrieking from the room.

Gaheries, meanwhile, came upon his brothers Gawain and Agravain, riding in the forest, and told them what had occurred. Gawain, raging, cried aloud that he would destroy Pellinore's son as he had destroyed Pellinore himself, and ever after the three brothers plotted to kill Sir Lamorack. ▷ 7TH JULY

3rd March

Joseph of Arimathea was a rich merchant who lived in Palestine at the time of the Passion of Jesus. Some said that he was Jesus' uncle by marriage, and that he had taken him to far-off places as a boy – for Joseph was a merchant with connections in the tin trade, which took him into distant corners of the Roman Empire. But no one knew if this was true or not, only that the Arimathean was almost certainly a secret follower of Jesus – the Christos as he was known. For when the terrible events of the Crucifixion took place Joseph went before Pilate the Roman, and asked that he be given the body of Jesus to place in his own tomb. Pilate agreed, though he made the condition that a guard of legionaries be placed upon the tomb. And it is said also that he gave Joseph the cup which had been used by Jesus to celebrate the Passover meal before his arrest, and that when Joseph assisted in the taking down of the body from the Cross, some blood flowed from the wound in Jesus' side, and that the Arimathean caught some of it in the cup – which was thereby made sacred forever, and became known in later times as the Holy Grail. ▷

4th March

After the events of the Resurrection Joseph was thrown into prison, where he was left to die of thirst and starvation. But as he lay one night in the darkness a great light appeared, and a Voice he recognized as belonging to Jesus spoke to him, saying that he was blessed among men and that he was to be the guardian of a great Mystery. And Joseph felt the shape of a Cup placed in his trembling hands, and certain words were whispered into his ear, which told of the secret uses of the Cup.

Thereafter, every evening a dove appeared in Joseph's cell bringing in its beak a wafer which it placed within the Cup. And this sustained Joseph through many days and weeks, until he thought himself forgotten. Then one day the door of his cell opened, and daylight entered, blinding him. A new Emperor now ruled in Rome, and he had been cured of a sickness by a holy relic. Therefore he sought out the Arimathean with intent to give him a proper burial – only to discover him still alive, and bearing in his hands an even greater thing. ▷

After the Deposition of Christ from the Cross, Joseph of Arimathea, depicted here with the Blessed Virgin Mary and St John, receives the Cup of the Last Supper, in which he catches some of the Saviour's blood. The vessel, thus hallowed, becomes known as the Holy Grail. (3rd March)

Hide: medieval measure of land, between 60 and 120 acres

5th March

So it came to pass that Joseph was set free. Gathering about him a band of faithful followers, he set forth for a distant land, where he had once travelled with the young Jesus, a place named Britain. After many months of sailing, and many more of travelling, Joseph and his party arrived at a place named in the old tongue Ynys Witrin, which is to say The Island of Glass, and there he was welcomed by the holy Druids, who knew of his coming. They gave Joseph twelve hides of land from their sacred enclosure, and granted him leave to build a chapel for the Cup.   ▷ 13th November

6th March

Gawain at last discovered the pavilion of the evil knight who had carried off the Lord of the Castle of Enquiry's son. But he came too late, for the youth was already dead. Gawain and the knight fought and Gawain slew the killer. Then he took up the youth's body and returned with it to his host. The king wept

and ordered that the body be placed in a great cauldron and boiled – everyone there was to receive a piece of the flesh. Recoiling from this custom, Gawain returned to the fountain and finding the hermit still there asked him to explain the procession he had seen earlier. The hermit said merely that he could not reveal 'the Secrets of the Saviour', save only to him that was destined to find the Grail – from which Gawain knew that it was not to be he. Yet he continued his quest and had many more adventures before the achieving of the Grail.

▷ 2ND SEPTEMBER

─────────── 7th March ───────────

Tristan and Isolt took ship from Ireland, and with them went Isolt's faithful handmaid Brangane, who had been entrusted with a certain potion by Isolt's mother. She suspected that her daughter's affections lay elsewhere than with her intended husband, so she made a potion that was to be administered to the couple on their wedding night, which would ensure that both loved each other as much as they might. But as fortune fell out, while the ship was at sea between the two lands, Brangane suffered greatly from sea-sickness and spent most of the time below decks. Tristan and Isolt, however, sat on deck, playing endless games of chess. When they grew thirsty Tristan went below in search of wine and, finding the vessel with the potion, brought that. And there upon the deck they pledged each other. Thus the two, who were already in love, drank the potion intended for Isolt and Mark, and conceived such a passion for each other that not even death could break.

▷ 12TH MARCH

─────────── 8th March ───────────

As Lancelot's fame spread so the number of evil men who wished him dead grew. One day as he rode along he saw a hawk fly overhead and land at the top of a tall tree, where its jesses became entangled so that it hung upside down from a branch, screeching furiously. A lady came in sight and begged Lancelot, in the name of his knighthood, to climb the tree and rescue her bird. And because he had vowed to refuse no honest request, Lancelot took off all his armour and climbed up. While he was in the tree the lady drew forth a bow and shot him in the left buttock. Angered by the pain and ignominy, Lancelot climbed down again, only to be attacked by the lady's husband, who had been lying in wait for this moment. Despite being unarmed and wounded, Lancelot knocked the man down and, snatching up his sword, beheaded him in a single stroke. The woman wept and wailed, fearing for her own life, but Lancelot spared her and demanded that she take him to a nearby hermitage where his wound could be dressed.

─────── ◇ ───────

JESSES: REINS BY WHICH A HAWK IS TETHERED

─────── ◇ ───────

While engaged in a chess game on the deck of the
ship taking them to Cornwall, Tristan and Isolt,
seeking refreshment, accidentally drink a potion
which is intended for the wedding night of Isolt and
King Mark of Cornwall. The two become lovers
thereafter. Brangane, Isolt's confidante, is also in the
picture behind the Princess. (7th March)

42

9th March

A knight of Arthur's court, named Trojan, who believed himself a great hunter, one day offered a wager to Gawain, pledging to bring back to court the finest piece of game anyone had ever seen. Gawain laughingly accepted and the two rode forth. Trojan soon returned with a deer of surpassing whiteness, which he presented to Guinevere. Gawain meanwhile rode into the wood. At sunrise he encountered a fearsome serpent and at once began to battle against it. Yet despite all his strength he could not so much as wound it, while it beat him to the ground. Then Gawain prepared to die, but the serpent suddenly spoke in a gentle voice: 'Do not weep, sir knight. I shall not kill you. Only tell me your name.' And Gawain, ashamed at being so easily beaten, said: 'I am Sir Lancelot.' But the serpent whispered: 'I have encountered that one already, and you are a much better fighter than he. Tell me your true name, for there is a knight I have loved these long years and if you are he then I shall give you such pleasure as you will never have again.' Then Gawain said his real name and at once the serpent vanished: in its place stood a beautiful woman who cast her arms around his neck and kissed him with passion. 'Ah Gawain, it is you. I am the daughter of Morgain le Fay. She put me in serpent shape to keep all men from me – yet I knew that when my true lover came I should be released by him!'   ▷

10th March

In the morning Gawain remembered his wager, and was dismayed that now he would have no rare beast with which to return to court. But the maiden gave him a ring. 'While you wear this you shall have any thing you desire, as long as you tell no one whence it came.' So Gawain set off back to Camelot, and as he rode he asked various things of the ring: a new suit of armour to replace his own which had been scorched by the serpent; a new horse; twenty hostage knights to present to King Arthur; and lastly a new kind of creature with the hooves of a griffin in front and those of a horse behind, with a fish's tail and peacock's wings, a woman's face and one black eye and one white eye. Such a beast had never been seen before, and caused much excited comment among all those gathered at the court to witness the result of the wager. When Gawain presented it to Guinevere he was at once pronounced the winner.

But Sir Trojan was eaten with jealousy, and by a trick he forced Gawain to say how he came by the creature. As Gawain confessed the story of the serpent and the ring a great cry echoed across the leagues of the forest, and for a moment the shadowy form of the maiden stood before Gawain before it dispersed like a mist. Never again did he see her, and it is said that Morgain imprisoned her in a cave beneath the sea.

*T*hough Arthur had put down the rebellion of the twelve kings, still there were those who murmured against him. He spoke of this to Merlin, and after a little thought the wise Mage said: 'Let you command the making of a great table, round in the likeness of the world, with one hundred and fifty sieges, and then call men from every kingdom to come and sit there. Thus shall all be equal in the sight of each other, and none seen to have more favour than the rest.' And Arthur did as Merlin told him. And Merlin had the sieges made with the names of those who would sit there – and the names that appeared in letters of gold were of men but lately born. But one seat remained blank, and a cloth covered it. This was the Siege Perilous, that only one destined to achieve the Quest of the Grail might sit in – but none knew of that save Merlin himself at that time.

SIEGE: SEAT

At the inauguration of the Round Table letters appear spelling the names of those knights intended to sit there. Here Arthur is showing them to their places.

---— 12th March ---—

Despite the love that was now indissolubly between them, Tristan brought Isolt safely to Cornwall and to Mark, who must now keep his promise to his barons and marry the owner of the golden hair. At the wedding Tristan in agony watched Isolt go through the ceremony like one in a dream. The wedding night loomed large, and the lovers knew that Mark would discover that his bride was no virgin. And so they hit upon a plan: Isolt asked her faithful handmaid, Brangane, to change places with her mistress once the candles were doused in the wedding chamber. And so it was done. Mark, who had drunk enough wine to ensure he knew nothing, clumsily took what was his right, never guessing that the woman in his arms was not Isolt – who lay elsewhere that night, and knew greater joy than her servant. ▷ 21ST JANUARY

---— 13th March ---—

A great wonder appeared in the sky over Camelot. Two suns shone, the like of which no one had seen before. Arthur called his sister to him to know what this might mean. Morgain said, 'Be advised, King and brother, that mighty events come to trouble this land. Prepare for a great joy and a great sorrow.' And she would say no more. ▷

---— 14th March ---—

The next day came a maiden with a sealed coffer into the court. 'Inside this coffer is a head. No one can open it save he who killed the one within.' This adventure was so dubious that Arthur himself had to try it first, but the coffer remained stubbornly closed. Since the King had tried, all other knights were bound to do so. Only Kay, Arthur's steward, had not tried. He came forward, indignant at being forgotten. 'I would all the heads of all the knights I ever slew, save one, were within so that you knew my worth.' The coffer fell open at his touch and letters fell out. The maiden read them: 'Here is the head of Loholt, son of Arthur and Guinevere, slain by Kay.' Guinevere fainted at the sight of the head and Kay was taken to the dungeon to be tried on the morrow. ▷

---— 15th March ---—

Arthur sat in solemn justice to hear the defence of his foster-brother. Kay stammered his sorry tale: 'Upon my last quest I encountered a giant who made me play a beheading game. I knew the way of it, I thought, since Gawain's contest those many Christmases ago. Instead of himself, the giant sent forth

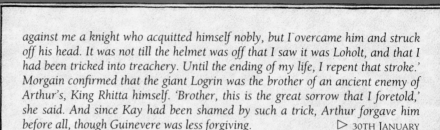

against me a knight who acquitted himself nobly, but I overcame him and struck off his head. It was not till the helmet was off that I saw it was Loholt, and that I had been tricked into treachery. Until the ending of my life, I repent that stroke.' Morgain confirmed that the giant Logrin was the brother of an ancient enemy of Arthur's, King Rhitta himself. 'Brother, this is the great sorrow that I foretold,' she said. And since Kay had been shamed by such a trick, Arthur forgave him before all, though Guinevere was less forgiving. ▷ 30TH JANUARY

16th March

*O*f all the earliest knights at Arthur's court the strongest, and also the most troublesome, were the brothers Balin and Balan. Balin especially had an evil reputation, having slain one of Arthur's cousins – for which he was imprisoned for six months before the King let him out again. He was still at court when a damsel appeared girt about with a sword that seemed very heavy for her. It was, she said, a marvellous weapon which only the destined man could draw forth. Many tried, and at length Balin himself took a turn. To everyone's astonishment he succeeded. But scarcely had he done so than a second lady entered and demanded either Balin's head or that of the first damsel who had brought the sword. Balin, overhearing her, struck off her head in front of the whole court. He then told how she had caused his mother to be burned as a witch. Arthur was too angry to listen to the story and banished Balin from his sight, and later from the court itself. ▷

17th March

*M*ore trouble followed Balin, in the shape of a hotheaded young knight named Lanceor, who set out in pursuit with the intention of pleasing Arthur and teaching the banished Balin a lesson. When they met, however, it was Lanceor who fell. His love Columb, finding him dead, fell prostrate beside him and expired. Balin's brother Balan found them there later, and sadly helped to bury them in a single grave. Then the brothers rode on together until they came to a parting of the ways and Balin rode one way while Balan rode the other. ▷

18th March

*B*alin next met with a knight named Herlews and his lady, with whom he rode for a day. But as they went Herlews was suddenly set upon and slain by an invisible opponent. Balin and the lady followed the track of the unseen rider, but in vain, and in due course they arrived at the castle of King Pelles.

At supper that evening Balin noticed a man who struck another for the slightest of reasons, and on asking his name was told it was Garlon, the King's brother, whom all men feared because of his ability to ride invisibly. Realizing this was the man they had been following, Balin rushed up to him and slew him with no warning, then fled through the castle when his sword broke in the first exchange of blows.

Running for dear life, he found himself in a richly appointed chamber where a wondrous Cup stood upon an altar and a mighty Spear hung on the wall. Snatching this up, Balin turned at bay and, as King Pelles entered, struck him through both thighs. And as the King fell the walls of the castle trembled and shook and then came crashing down, killing many of the people, including Herlews' lady, and burying Balin.   ▷

—————— 19th March ——————

*I*n the morning Merlin came and pulled Balin from the ruin. 'This was an evil deed,' he said. 'That spear was the lance with which the legionary Longinus pierced the side of the Lord Christ as he hung upon the Rood. Because of what you have done King Pelles will suffer the wound until the day when the mysteries of the Grail are achieved. And this shall be called the Dolorous Blow, for all the lands about here are henceforth laid waste and thus they will remain until the Cup of the Lord is poured out upon the land.'   ▷

ROOD: CRUCIFIX

—————— 20th March ——————

*B*alin went his way, and everywhere he saw ruined fields and dry rivers, and people who saw him cursed him. At length he found himself at a castle where the custom was that whatever knight came there must do battle with the guardian of an island close by.

Balin had lost both shield and helm and these were provided for him before he departed. As he rode he heard a hunting horn winding the mort and he said: 'Alas, for that horn sounds for me.' But still he continued, and at the island met and fought with the guardian. All day the battle continued, until at length both men fell wounded to death. Then Balin took off his helmet and helped the other knight off with his. And he saw that it was his own brother Balan, who had defeated the previous guardian and taken his armour.

Later Merlin came and had them buried in a single tomb, which he marked with a great stone; the magical sword which Balin had from the lady he took and set aside until the coming of Galahad, when it next appeared floating in a block of marble outside Camelot.

MORT: DEATH OF THE QUARRY

47

21st March

It was at his coronation that Uther first looked upon Igrain, the wife of Gorlois of Cornwall. From that moment, he could think of no other woman. Gorlois perceived Uther's lust and withdrew himself and his wife to his castle at Tintagel. The castle was set on the seaward side, the only access being by way of a postern. Uther's suffering was such that Merlin agreed to help him. By use of his otherworldly arts, Merlin gave Uther the semblance of Gorlois so that when the King rode up to the postern gate the men at arms opened it, seeing, as they supposed, their Duke. So it was that Uther spent the night with Igrain, she all unknowing of the deception, so skilful was the semblance of Gorlois upon the King. That night was Arthur Pendragon conceived. ▷ 20TH DECEMBER

22nd March

In Arthur's time the King of Wales was named Caradoc. He had two offspring, Meriadoc and Orwen, who were both still children when their father was murdered by his brother Griffith. This evil man then declared himself king and paid two henchmen to take the children into the forest and kill them. When the moment came, however, they were unable to do the deed but instead gave them into the care of Ivor, the late King's huntsman. He brought them up well, never allowing them to forget their father or their true lineage. ▷

23rd March

One day Uriens of Gore happened to visit. He took one look at Orwen and fell in love with her. Next morning he had gone, and the girl with him. Soon after, Ivor took Meriadoc to King Arthur and laid the boy's claim before him. Kay took him as his squire. Meanwhile Arthur commanded Griffith to appear before him, and when he failed to do so declared war on him. He was joined in this venture by Uriens, who still loved the fair Orwen and had learned of her true identity. Griffith soon capitulated and was summarily executed, Meriadoc being declared king in his place. But the young Prince had his mind on errantry, and gave over his kingdom to Uriens to rule it in his sister's name. ▷

24th March

Meriadoc wandered through the world, fighting as a mercenary, carving out a name for himself beyond the realm of Arthur's lands. He returned at last after he had been deprived of the hand of a Gaulish princess by a powerful rival, no less than the King of Gaul himself. Then word reached him that this same

---◇---

ERRANTRY: WANDERING IN
SEARCH OF ADVENTURE

---◇---

Princess had been refused by her intended husband when it was discovered that she was pregnant by Meriadoc; he returned to Gaul and married his love, being given a position of power in his old rival's own realm. From there he continued to rule, becoming a strong ally of Arthur in years to come. Uriens in time put Orwen aside for the powerful charms of the lady Morgain, and the Princess ruled alone in her own lands until she married a man who bore her father's name, Caradoc, with whom she lived a contented life.

25th March

The three remaining Grail knights came at last to Sarras, the Holy City, where they disembarked and carried the Grail to its destined home. Josephus, the son of Joseph of Arimathea, welcomed Galahad like a brother – for he too had been of an earlier Grail fellowship. They talked for a long while concerning their mysterious adventures.

And if Galahad had seemed more than a mortal man while on the Ship of Solomon, now he appeared to shine as though illumined like light through crystal. Bors and Perceval were in great dread of their companion, but Galahad allayed their fears. 'My friends, our adventures are over for this time. We have shared much together and, of all King Arthur's knights, we alone were found worthy to achieve the quest for the Holy Grail. When you return, men will wonder for a little while and amend their lives for a space, but soon enough things will be as they were before and the Grail will be forgotten. And so, my friends and brothers, you must remember and tell this quest when men grow forgetful.'

Then Perceval embraced him. 'I knew you would not come home with us. God grant that we meet again.' 'Amen,' said Galahad. And, turning to Bors, who stood amazed and fearful, he said gently: 'It will be but a short while before we do. Sir Bors, as soon as you see my father Sir Lancelot, greet him for me.'

Then the three friends embraced one last time as men, for before their eyes Bors and Perceval felt Galahad slip from them into death. Their grief was no less heavy than if they had lost their friend in some battle instead of in this gentle and holy place. They buried him there, together with Perceval's sister Dindrane, and took ship again for Arthur's realm.   ▷

26th March

'Having seen the shores of the Holy City, I cannot rest in the courts of men,' said Perceval, and afterwards he became a hermit in the woods, a guide to travellers in search of spiritual quests. Bors went with him and remained for a short time before returning to Camelot to recount all that had passed to King

Arthur. All the court wondered greatly with a mixture of joy and sorrow, joy for the marvels that had been achieved, and sorrow for the many knights who were lost. And Bors greeted Sir Lancelot from his son Sir Galahad, turning away as he saw the tears in the great knight's eyes.

27th March

Arthur announced one day: 'I go now to Ireland, for I must convene the chase of the Dangerous Forest, which it is my destiny to perform every seventh year. Who goes with me?' The knights clamoured for notice, but Arthur took with him only forty-eight of their number. ▷

28th March

While they sat about the fire in the Dangerous Forest, a wondrous champion called the Knight of the Lantern appeared, who mocked Arthur and the prowess of the Round Table and challenged each knight to combat. Each one he overcame and bound, until only Arthur and his young squire Gwalchaved remained. 'I come again, King Arthur,' said the Knight of the Lantern, and left the two alone surrounded by a magical mist. 'What shame upon us!' said Arthur. 'If our enemies knew of our predicament, the Round Table's honour would be naught. Now I am bereft of knights.' 'Not so, lord,' said Gwalchaved and he begged Arthur to knight him so that, boy though he was, he might bring help. 'If there be any man of Adam's race that will assist us, find him and bring him here,' said Arthur. He knighted Gwalchaved and bade him go with God. ▷

29th March

Gwalchaved stumbled about the forest until he came to a clearing where a giant dog with no ears stood, its eyes full of moonlight. 'What is the news?' said the dog in a human voice. Gwalchaved almost ran away with fright, but remembered that he was now Arthur's knight. The dog saw that he was but a young boy and spoke kindly, 'Tell me the news and I shall aid you.' And Gwalchaved told what had befallen. 'This is great news, for none but I can fight the Knight of the Lantern, and it is my destiny to overcome him or remain in this shape.' And Gwalchaved rode upon the dog's back all the way to where Arthur and his men lay bound with the bonds of magic. 'Tell us how you gained this shape and what help you can bring us,' said Arthur to the crop-eared dog. The dog crossed its paws and told how he was born Alastrann, the son of the King of India. His stepmother had borne the Knight of the Lantern and wished him to

Arthur fights the Cornish giant while his men look on. Also
depicted in this illustration, though not in the story, is a
giantess, who looks on placidly while her mate is attacked
by Arthur. (31st March)

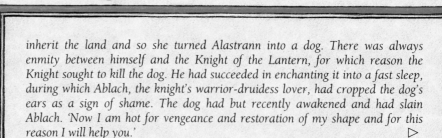

inherit the land and so she turned Alastrann into a dog. There was always enmity between himself and the Knight of the Lantern, for which reason the Knight sought to kill the dog. He had succeeded in enchanting it into a fast sleep, during which Ablach, the knight's warrior-druidess lover, had cropped the dog's ears as a sign of shame. The dog had but recently awakened and had slain Ablach. 'Now I am hot for vengeance and restoration of my shape and for this reason I will help you.' ▷

—————— 30th March ——————

*A*rthur and Gwalchaved waited until the Knight of the Lantern returned and then, letting loose the great dog's leash, Gwalchaved set Alastrann upon him. One stroke of his mighty paw opened up the knight's chest, and he begged for mercy. 'Only restore me to my rightful shape once more and swear to be my true vassal and I shall grant you life.' The Knight of the Lantern spoke the words of disenchantment and Alastrann stood as a man once more. At the same time the magical mist and bindings vanished and Arthur's knights found their lord and the newly-knighted Gwalchaved. Together with Alastrann, they took ship and sailed homewards to Britain.

—————— 31st March ——————

*A*rthur heard of a terrible giant who was terrorizing the neighbourhood along the coast of Kernow. Taking with him only Sir Bedivere and Sir Kay he set off at once for the place. They arrived at night near St Michael's Mount and there met a woman weeping and crying. She told them that the giant had but lately seized the Duchess of Brittany, and in forcing her to lie with him had slain her. Even now the monstrous creature was encamped close by. Bidding the others wait and comfort the woman, Arthur climbed the mount to where the giant's encampment lay. Soon he espied him, vast and gross, seated by a fire over which two weeping maidens turned a spit on which were the bodies of five newborn children. In anger and horror Arthur rushed out and struck the giant without warning. Roaring, the creature snatched up his club and struck at the King, who dodged and delivered a fearsome wound to the creature's belly. Bellowing in agony the giant threw down his club, seized Arthur and began to squeeze his ribs. Arthur would certainly have perished, had not the giant's foot slipped on the grass and the two rolled over and over to the bottom of the mount. As they rolled Arthur managed to draw his dagger and thrust it repeatedly into the giant's body. When they arrived at the bottom the giant was dead, though it took all the efforts of Sir Bedivere and Sir Kay to free the King from his embrace.

————— ◇ —————

KERNOW: CORNWALL

————— ◇ —————

APRIL

Lovers who are very often able to have each
other's company are apt to imagine that some
other is more loved than they, and they will
make a great quarrel out of a caprice, and for
a tiff will make peace right royally. And there
is good reason why they should do so. We
must uphold them in this, since affection will
grow rich, young, and fresh from it, and take
fire in its attachment. On the other hand, it
grows poor, old, cold and frigid when it lacks
its fire; when anger is spent, affection does
not quickly grow green again. But when
lovers fall out over a trifle it is loyalty, fresh
and ever new, that will always be the
peacemaker. This renews their loyalty, this
refines their affection like gold.

Gottfried von Strassburg: Tristan

1st April

One day as the Knights of the Round Table were preparing to sit down to dinner, a young and handsome squire entered the hall and begged a boon of King Arthur – that he be given the first adventure that came to hand. While Arthur was still pondering this request a knight all visored in black rode full-tilt into the hall, drove the point of his lance through the breast of a knight who sat unarmed at table, and with a scornful laugh rode out again, crying: 'Thus shall I do every month until there are none of you left.' At once a dozen knights rose to pursue him, but the young squire renewed his plea. 'Who are you?' demanded Arthur. 'Sire,' the young man answered eagerly, 'I am the son of Dovon, your true knight, and my name is Griflet.' And Arthur, remembering the old knight as a brave and good man, granted Griflet's request, and the noble youth set forth at once on his quest.   ▷

2nd April

After many weeks of travelling and as many adventures upon the way, Griflet met a woman on the road, whose torn garments and reddened eyes told their own story. Questioned, she told a tale of horror. A company of lepers had taken refuge in an old castle nearby and were terrorizing the neighbourhood, stealing children, in whose blood they bathed to hold at bay their terrible sickness. At once Griflet set himself towards the castle and found the nest of evil men, whom he slew unhesitatingly. All save one lay dead, and he crawled on the ground begging for mercy. Griflet sought out the prisoners and the children not yet killed, but the door to the prison was held by powerful enchantment, and when Griflet questioned the wounded leper he was told that he must find a certain marble head in the tower of the castle and destroy it. This he did, shattering the skull with a single blow. It screamed aloud and half the castle fell at once in ruins, burying the last of the lepers and freeing the imprisoned villagers and their children. All thanked Griflet and one among them was able to tell him where the black knight, Taulat of Rugimon, lived. Griflet set out for the place at once.

▷ 22ND APRIL

3rd April

One day Lancelot came to where a fair meadow stretched, with a shady tree and a trickling stream, and being hot and tired he lay down to sleep, putting aside his armour and weapons. And while he slept there came four Queens: Morgain le Fay, Queen of Gore, Morgause of Orkney, the Queen of Norgalles and the Queen of the East Lands. When they saw the great knight sleeping, cheek

upon palm, Morgain le Fay at once cast a spell upon him, and when he awoke he found himself in a deep dungeon, with no memory of how he came there. Soon there came to him a fair damsel who greeted him kindly and gave him to eat. But when Lancelot asked where he was she could only shake her head in warning and bid him be of good cheer. ▷

─────────────── 4th April ───────────────

Next morning there came into his cell the four Queens, and when Lancelot saw that one of them was Morgain le Fay he knew his fears well founded. 'Sir Lancelot,' said she, 'you know me well, I think. These other ladies are Queens also. One of us you must have for your mistress, or else die.' Lancelot looked back at her and answered: 'Madam, I fear then that I must die, for you know well that I can love no woman.' Angrily the four Queens departed, promising to return the next day. Shortly afterwards the fair maiden came in again bearing a tray of food. And as she set it down she again bade Lancelot be of good cheer, and said to him softly, 'Be sure that I shall find a way to set you free.' Then she was gone, and Lancelot was left alone. ▷

─────────────── 5th April ───────────────

Next morning, again the four Queens appeared and again made the same offer, and were again refused. After they had departed the maiden came in again, and with finger to lips led Sir Lancelot out of the dungeon and to the door of the castle. There she said: 'As I have helped you, so must you help me. My father, King Bagdemagus, fights in a tournament close at hand. For three days now he has lost because of the Round Table knights who fight against him. Go, take his side and make the score more even.' Lancelot did as he was bid, out of gratitude to the maiden, and indeed his presence turned the tide in favour of her father, for Lancelot rode incognito in the tournament and as always none could stand against him. But Morgain le Fay forgave him not and ever plotted to destroy him from that moment.

─────────────── 6th April ───────────────

One day as Arthur, Gawain and other knights of the Round Table were riding in the forest, they heard the cries of a distressed maiden and hurried to her aid. They found her standing at the edge of a field of corn, watching in dismay as a vast brown bull wandered hither and thither tearing and crushing the crop. Arthur smiled: 'Let me deal with this,' he said, and dismounting from his proud

(Left) Lancelot sleeps beneath a tree while three otherworldly Queens and their retainers approach. In most versions of the story there are four Queens, but here the artist has had room for only three. As in many illustrations of this period, several of the faces remain unfinished. (3rd April)

(Below) After he has overcome the enchantments of the Lost Forest (in the first frame of this medieval strip), Lancelot's final task is to play a game with a magical chessboard. Winning, he sends it to Guinevere who, in the final frame, is shown playing with Arthur. (8th April)

57

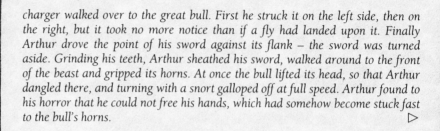

charger walked over to the great bull. First he struck it on the left side, then on the right, but it took no more notice than if a fly had landed upon it. Finally Arthur drove the point of his sword against its flank – the sword was turned aside. Grinding his teeth, Arthur sheathed his sword, walked around to the front of the beast and gripped its horns. At once the bull lifted its head, so that Arthur dangled there, and turning with a snort galloped off at full speed. Arthur found to his horror that he could not free his hands, which had somehow become stuck fast to the bull's horns. ▷

7th April

*T*he creature galloped straight to a tall rock, which it climbed with unnatural agility. There it stopped, its head jutting over the edge so that Arthur dangled there, helpless. Gawain and the rest of the knights clustered anxiously. Kay stared up at the King and suggested that all of them remove their cloaks and lay them in a heap on the ground to break Arthur's fall. As it saw this the beast began slowly to shake its head from side to side, while those below grew more anxious with every second. Then suddenly the bull sprang backwards and, rising onto its hind legs, became a tall man in a cloak of scarlet and rich attire. 'Have no fear, my lord,' he laughed, 'I am Mabonagrain. I mean you no harm. This was but a jest.' 'A jest I could ill do with,' said Arthur ruefully. 'Still, I forgive you, sir. Will you attend upon me at my court?' 'I shall be glad to do so,' said Mabonagrain, and when the knights had collected their cloaks the whole party returned laughing and joking to Camelot.*

8th April

*O*nce Lancelot braved the dangers of the Lost Forest, a place of strange, otherworldly magic. His reward was a magical chessboard, whose pieces moved of their own accord. He sent the board to Guinevere who played several games with Arthur, but, despite her every effort, lost each one.

9th April

*A*s the fame of Arthur's court grew it became customary for noblemen to send their sons to be educated there. One such was Gliglois, a young man of great charm and simplicity whose ways won the hearts of most people he met. The one exception was a lady named Beauté, whom he loved deeply but who spurned his clumsy advances, preferring to set herself at Gawain, whose squire Gliglois had become. ▷

10th April

One morning as Gliglois was in the garden feeding his master's falcons Beauté came out also. She was struggling to lace up her chemise and imperiously commanded the squire to help. With trembling fingers Gliglois obeyed, and when his eyes finally met hers he found Beauté smiling. 'How you tremble!' she said. 'Lady, I … It is only because of your presence,' confessed Gliglois, blushing mightily, and in a rush of words stammered forth his protestation of love. At once Beauté's smiles turned to frowns and she pulled away from him, furiously telling him to leave her in peace and cease his babbling. Hurt, Gliglois retreated. In the days that followed he became so miserable that Gawain noticed and demanded the reason. When Gliglois confessed all the knight offered to speak to Beauté on his behalf. But when the moment came Gawain seemed more interested in pressing his own suit rather than Gliglois', and promised to wear her favour in a forthcoming tournament.   ▷

11th April

On the day of the jousts all the ladies set forth escorted by their knights. But Beauté lacked an escort and, refusing Gliglois' tentative offer, haughtily demanded that he find one for her. This he did, not without a pang of jealousy; then, when the party set out, he walked with them. He walked all the way to the jousting field – some miles distant – in the heat of the day. More than once Beauté's escort offered to share his mount with the squire, but each time she sternly refused. At the tournament, however, fate took a turn. Gawain had wrenched a muscle in a practice joust earlier, and to Gliglois' astonishment insisted that he must ride in the lists instead, wearing his armour with Beauté's favour on it.   ▷

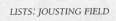

LISTS: JOUSTING FIELD

12th April

Gliglois, trembling in every limb, armed himself and went out to take part in the tournament. There he distinguished himself so well that many amid the throng believed he was Gawain. At the end of the day the young man was declared the winner in the jousts, and went forward to collect the prize, raising his visor so that all saw he was not Gawain. The King's nephew himself came limping on to the field and gave an explanation of all that had occurred. Beauté, smiling radiantly, took the first chance to speak with Gliglois. She confessed that she had admired him from the start, but had wanted to test him before she answered his suit. Now she confided her truer feelings, and the two were joyously married within the month.

13th April

Herzeloyde was the widow of Duke Evrawc. She had borne him six fair sons, all of whom were now dead in various wars, skirmishes and tournaments. For all such warlike activities Herzeloyde had conceived an utter detestation, and it was so that she came to live secluded in the forest, with only a handful of old retainers, to bear her husband's posthumous child, Perceval.

The boy was brought up in total ignorance of arms and chivalry, but his natural ebullience led him to fashion wooden darts with which to hunt game. Such was his foolishness that once, while herding his mother's goats, he captured two hinds, believing them to be goats which had lost their horns. And all were amazed, not only at his foolishness, but at his swiftness and strength. ▷

14th April

On another occasion, while casting at birds one day, he heard a great commotion in the forest. Hurrying in the direction of the sound, Perceval saw riding towards him three beings of unsurpassed glory: sunlight flashed on their shining apparel and the woods rang with the jingling of their splendid harness. Perceval believed they must be the angels his mother so often spoke of, and he knelt reverently in their path. Owain, Gawain and Geneir ap Gwystyl stopped dumbfounded before the great lad clad in patched raiment. 'Good angels, take me with you!' begged Perceval. Geneir tapped his head meaningfully at his companions, but Gawain leant out of the saddle and raised the boy and spoke kindly: 'We are not angels, lad; we are knights.' Perceval's face turned in wonder, 'What are knights?' Gawain, Owain and Geneir told Perceval something of the usages of knighthood and arms, and of the great Round Table instituted by King Arthur. Perceval was so fired by their speech that he sped home to ask his mother's permission to become a knight. ▷

15th April

Herzeloyde's heart was heavy as she saw her son ready to depart from their woodland seclusion. In her unworldly way, she offered Perceval advice that might be useful to him: 'Wherever you see a church, kneel and say a Paternoster. If you see meat and drink and none to offer you food, take what you need. If you hear an outcry, go speedily towards it, especially if it is a woman in distress. If you see a fair jewel, take it and win honour by giving it to another. If you see a fair woman, pay court to her and you will be better esteemed by all.' Perceval stayed only to kiss his mother and mount upon the miserable nag that was their only horse; he rode away uncaring of all save knighthood. ▷ 4TH FEBRUARY

16th April

Dionas was a good squire of the Duke of Brittany. He held the Goddess Diana in great honour and made prayers to her at the full moon. It was so that Diana appeared to him and promised that he should have a daughter who would win the heart of the greatest magician in the world. And in time Dionas indeed had a daughter by one of the Lady of the Lake's maidens, and the child was called Nimue.

▷ 1ST AUGUST

17th April

It was Arthur's custom that none should eat until there had appeared a great wonder as all sat at the Round Table. This day there came into court a white hart and a white brachet. The brachet bit the rump of the white hart and then jumped into a knight's lap. He went out with the animal. Immediately there entered a lady on a white palfrey. She called loudly to King Arthur: 'Sire, give me

◇

NIMUE: SOMETIMES REFERRED TO AS VIVIEN

◇

◇

BRACHET: HUNTING DOG

◇

The Quest for the White Hart was the first adventure of the Round Table. Here two knights are shown following it; also seen is the dog which had been carried off by another knight.

◇

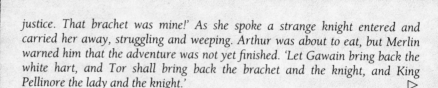

justice. That brachet was mine!' As she spoke a strange knight entered and carried her away, struggling and weeping. Arthur was about to eat, but Merlin warned him that the adventure was not yet finished. 'Let Gawain bring back the white hart, and Tor shall bring back the brachet and the knight, and King Pellinore the lady and the knight.' ▷

----------- 18th April -----------

Gawain rode in search of the white hart, chasing it into a nearby castle. He arrived in time to see a knight, Sir Ablamar, emerge with bloody sword, lamenting that he had slain the white hart given him by his sovereign lady. Gawain saw that Ablamar had also killed his hounds, and he was so angry that he made to behead the knight, who knelt weeping. Just then, a lady came from the chamber and, falling over Ablamar, by chance caught Gawain's axe-stroke. The knight's companions were all for slaying Gawain, but their four ladies begged mercy for him and laid on him the task of returning to court with the white hart's head. They also made him ride with the lady's head about his neck and her body over his crupper. Arthur was greatly angered and passed Gawain over to the mercy of the ladies of the court, who charged him with being ever their champion and never again offending a lady in anything. ▷

----------- 19th April -----------

Tor rode in search of the brachet and the knight who had borne it away. He found the dog in a tent where a lady slept. With the urgency of quest upon him, he took up the brachet and was immediately attacked by the lady's knight, Sir Abelleus. Tor overcame him and bade him yield, but Abelleus refused. Just then a maiden rode up and asked a favour in Arthur's name: the head of Abelleus who had slain her brother. Since Abelleus had refused to yield, Tor beheaded him and returned to court, to the approbation of his King. ▷ 15TH MAY

----------- 20th April -----------

After the rebellion of the twelve kings had been put down days of peace followed, and Arthur's loyal barons demanded that he take a wife. Calling Merlin to him, Arthur bade him journey to the castle of King Leodegraunce of Cameliarde: 'For I love his daughter, Guinevere, and since I must take a wife to help maintain my kingdom, I will have none but she.' And Merlin was troubled by this, for being able to see into the mists of time he foresaw the secret love which would arise between Lancelot and Arthur's bride. Therefore he begged Arthur to

choose another lady. But in his youth and strength the King would have none of it, but sent Merlin to Leodegraunce to make a settlement. Guinevere's father was well pleased with so high a match for his daughter, but it seemed to Guinevere herself that Arthur's counsellor, the Mage with his all-seeing mind, looked upon her with long, mournful eyes which filled her days with disquiet and her nights with confused dreams.   ▷

─────────────── 21st April ───────────────

*A*t last all was set in readiness. To do honour to his intended wife Arthur sent the best of his knights, Lancelot du Lac, to lead the wedding party which would escort her to Camelot. He sent messages of love and tokens of future affection by means of his friend and companion-in-arms.

Clothed in beauty like the Queen of the May, Guinevere received her escort and listened to his courtly messages. But on the tongue of Lancelot Arthur's messages took on a fresh meaning. The King's friend and the King's bride looked upon each other with love. 'Lady, I pledge myself your champion from this day forward,' said Lancelot, speaking for himself now. And the promises which husband and wife give to each other in the sacrament of love were exchanged between them in their hearts. And though each accepted all that duty would demand – that Guinevere be faithful to Arthur and Lancelot his faithful knight – the day would come when love itself would master duty.   ▷ 19TH MAY

─────────────── 22nd April ───────────────

*F*or more than a year Griflet searched for Taulat. By chance, when he was utterly weary, he came to where a fair orchard lay, sheltered by high walls, and there he rested, sinking at once into a deep sleep. He was awoken by a servant who demanded that he present himself to the lady Brunnisend, the owner of the orchard. So tired was Griflet that he refused. Finally seven men came and seized him as he lay and carried him into the hall, where he found himself face to face with the most beautiful woman he had ever seen. Apologizing for his earlier behaviour, Griflet was made welcome – he was already half in love with the lady. But during the evening, as a bell rang for sunset, all the court began to cry out in great sorrow. When Griflet asked the reason for this he found himself set upon by a dozen men and beaten almost senseless. In the morning he arose and departed early without even taking his leave, and so continued on his way.

Arriving at another castle, he found an old knight who had been a companion to his father. From him he learned that Taulat's castle lay but an hour's ride distant, and also the reason for the sorrow of his recent hosts – their

63

lord was a captive of Taulat, who every month, when the poor man's wounds were healed, had him whipped and beaten so that they opened again, and thus he was kept in permanent suffering.

Outraged at this fresh evidence of Taulat's evil nature, Griflet rode fast to his destination and there challenged Taulat to combat. He, arrogantly, declared that he would meet the youth with no more defence than a shield and spear – but soon regretted it as Griflet felled him, wounded near to death, in a single joust.

Magnanimously, Griflet spared the life of the evil knight, though he died soon after from his wounds. Brunnisend's father he set free, and so ended the evil that had hung over that place. Brunnisend he later married, and sent word to Arthur that his knight was avenged.

———— 23rd April ————

Arthur held court at the castle of Kenadonne, close to the marches of Wales. As was the custom the court would not sit down to dinner until they had seen a marvel. Sir Gawain, looking out of a window, saw three men on horseback approaching with a dwarf who went on foot. He watched the men dismount, and saw that one was taller by a span than the others, but walked leaning upon their shoulders. 'Now prepare the feast,' he said, 'for I believe that here we have our wonder.'

The three men came into the court, the tall one, who was young, well made and handsome of face, leaning upon the shoulders of the others. As they came before Arthur, the youth drew himself upright with ease and said: 'Fair Lord, I

Gareth of Orkney arrives at Arthur's court incognito, and there requests that he be given food and lodging for a year. Disappointed, Arthur hands him over to Sir Kay, who sets him to work in the kitchens.

crave a boon.' 'Ask,' said Arthur. 'Sire, I ask that you give me food and lodging for one year, at which time I shall ask for two further gifts.' 'Ask for something more than this,' Arthur said, 'for this is but a simple thing that any man might give.' But the youth would not be moved. Nor would he give his name, and Arthur, disappointed, handed him over to Sir Kay. He, bitter-tongued as ever, chose to interpret the request in his own way. 'Well,' he said, looking at the youth, 'If it's food you require you shall have it – in the kitchens. You shall work there for a year. For I daresay you are a low-born churl.' So the youth became a kitchen knave for a time, and because of his large, unusually white hands, Kay named him 'Beaumains' which means 'Fair Hands'.   ▷ 10TH AUGUST

CHURL: PEASANT

—————— 24th April ——————

*F*inally Lancelot came to Rigomer. The castle was defended by a formidable array of dangers – invincible knights, a dragon with poisoned claws – but the knowledge that many prisoners lay within made Lancelot cunning in his strategy. He gained entrance but he was beguiled by a maiden carrying a golden apple. She gave him a ring, saying that the Lady Dionise, chatelaine of Castle Rigomer, had sent it to him as a love-token. As soon as he put it on, Lancelot became as a bestial slave. Whatever anyone asked of him, he would perform it. Thus he was set to work in the kitchens at the most menial tasks.   ▷ 2ND MAY

—————— 25th April ——————

*A*fter the death of Gorlois of Cornwall, his successor, Mark, paid tribute to the King of Ireland, who each year sent his champion, a gigantic warrior named Marhaus, to bring back twelve youths and maidens to serve as slaves at the Irish court. No one had ever dared challenge this custom until Tristan, Mark's nephew, newly come from Brittany, declared that it was a shame for the lords of Cornwall to continue paying such a tribute, and offered to stand against Marhaus himself.

On the day appointed the two warriors met on the Island of St Sampson, and there fought long and hard throughout the day, until at last Tristan dispatched his adversary with a mighty blow – but not before he received in turn a wound in the thigh from Marhaus' sword. His own blade left a splinter of steel embedded in the brain-pan of the Irish warrior.

Now unbeknown to Tristan, Marhaus' sword was poisoned, and though he returned to the court a hero, the wound would not heal, and soon began to rot. Then a wise woman advised that Tristan should be set adrift in a rudderless craft, which would either lead him to death or to one who could heal him.   ▷

26th April

For days the wounded Tristan was carried on the waves, delirious and weak, until the craft fetched up on the shore of Ireland. There fisherfolk found him and, seeing the terrible wound, sent for the King's daughter Isolt, who was famed throughout the land for her healing skills. She came at once, all unknowing that this was the slayer of her uncle, her father's champion. ▷

27th April

As he began to recover Tristan quickly learned who his healer was. He gave his name as 'Tantrist', and said that he was a wandering harper who had been attacked by pirates and set adrift. As Isolt nursed him back to health a friendship grew between them which soon ripened into love, though as yet unacknowledged by either. Then it happened that one day, as Tristan was taking a bath, Isolt chanced to catch sight of his sword in the adjacent room, and thinking to clean it she drew it forth. There she saw that a piece was missing from the blade, and with a low cry ran to where she had kept the splinter of steel from the wound of Marhaus. It fitted exactly. Now she knew the true identity of 'Tantrist', and lifting the sword above her head ran into the bath-chamber and would have slain him there. But as she looked upon him the hatred suddenly left her, to be replaced by love, and there and then the two confessed their passion.

Tristan remained in Ireland for a further six months, attending Isolt as a teacher of the harp. But gradually her mother, the Queen, began to suspect that he was the slayer of her brother, and so Isolt sent him away. Sadly the two exchanged rings before he departed for Cornwall. ▷ 7TH SEPTEMBER

28th April

As the feast of Pentecost approached the entire Fellowship of the Round Table began to assemble at Camelot. There came a lady seeking Sir Lancelot, and when she was shown where he sat, she approached him and asked that he come with her to a nearby abbey. 'For there is a youth that requires knighthood, and it is best that it comes from your hand alone, Sir Lancelot.' Used to such requests, Lancelot did his best not to refuse any, so he went with the lady. And at the abbey there came in twelve nuns and with them a youth of such beauty and strength that Lancelot stood amazed. 'Is this he that desires knighthood?' he demanded, and they said as one, 'Yes, it is he.' 'And is the wish his own?' 'It is.' 'Then I shall do as you all wish.'

So at the celebration of the Mass, Lancelot knighted the youth, whose name was Galahad, inviting him to the feast in four weeks' time. ▷ 31ST MAY

While tending Tristan's wounds Isolt discovers his sword, and from a nick in the blade recognizes it as the weapon which has slain her uncle Marhaus. She attacks Tristan in his bath, but cannot bring herself to kill him.

----------- 29th April -----------

Gawain loved many women, and married three, but the one he loved the best he lost most strangely. It came about that one day a knight named Joram appeared at Camelot in time for a tournament. He defeated every knight he encountered (Lancelot was absent so it is not known if he would have been beaten also). The last to fall was Gawain, and Joram declared that since, by the laws of chivalry, he was now his prisoner, Gawain must accompany him to his home. That proved to be a magical place, hidden behind a screen of mountains. There Gawain met Joram's daughter Florie, and at once fell deeply in love with her. Since the girl's father seemed pleased by this the two married, and Gawain stayed in Joram's kingdom for a year – long enough to see a son born, whom they named Gwigalois. But, despite the pleasures of life in the magical kingdom, Gawain began to be restless for the walls and towers of Camelot and the voices of his friends. He set off for home, leaving a ring to be given to his son should any ill befall him upon the way. ▷

----------- 30th April -----------

After a pleasurable period in the company of the knights of the Round Table, Gawain obtained permission from Arthur to return to his new wife. Confidently he set out to follow the path he had trodden twice now, but to his dismay could not find it. For a year he searched, growing thin and weary, encountering adventures which he pursued with single-minded grimness. But in all that time he saw neither sight nor sign of the pass through the mountains into Joram's kingdom.

Later a boy came knocking at the doors of Camelot, asking for Gawain. He was Gwigalois, grown to manhood with unearthly quickness, but he could tell no one, least of all his father, the way into his grandfather's realm. He was to become one of the greatest of the younger knights of the Round Table, with all his father's skill and his grandfather's unearthly power. Gawain mourned for Florie long years before he met another lady who captured his heart.

MAY

In May ... every lusty heart beginneth to blossom,
and to bring forth fruit; for like as herbs and trees
bring forth fruit and flourish in May, in like wise
every lusty heart that is in any manner a lover,
springeth and flourisheth in lusty deeds ... for then
all herbs and trees renew a man and woman, and
likewise lovers call again to their mind old gentleness
and service, and many kind deeds that were
forgotten by negligence ... Nowadays, men can not
love seven nights but they must have all their desires:
that love may not endure by reason ... Right so
fareth love nowadays, soon hot, soon cold: this is no
stability. But the old love was not so; men and
women could love together seven years and no
licours lusts were between them, and then was love,
truth, and faithfulness; and lo, in like wise was used
love in King Arthur's days.

Malory: Le Morte DArthur

1st May

As Queen Guinevere rode out Maying with ten of her knights and ladies of the court, she was accosted by Sir Melwas of the Summer Country, who professed great love for her. When she refused to go with him, his soldiers attacked the company of unarmed knights and ladies so that the Queen had to surrender herself or watch them die. Melwas permitted one of Guinevere's pages to escape in order that he might entrap and kill Lancelot, knowing that he would come as soon as word of the abduction reached him. ▷ 4TH MAY

2nd May

News came to Camelot that Lancelot was imprisoned in Castle Rigomer. When Gawain heard how this great knight, his friend, was so humbled, he gathered together a great company to rescue him. So indignant were the Round Table knights at this slight to their champion that no less than five hundred were ready to go. Arthur bade Gawain take fifty-eight and ride forth in rescue. ▷

3rd May

Gawain and his men became separated in their search for Lancelot. The other knights rode off to Rigomer, where they found themselves assailed by terrible enchantments. Gawain was himself captured by Gaudiones but he was able to escape with the help of the Fay Lorie, who aided his enterprise. Gawain had learned that only a knight of high renown could overcome the enchantments of Rigomer, for its lady, Dionise, could not be married until a knight of great skill and generosity came. Only then would the knights in her dungeon be liberated, and all wounded by the enchantments would be healed. ▷ 26TH FEBRUARY

4th May

Guinevere's page rode as fast as he could to find Sir Lancelot. 'Sir, the Queen has been abducted by Sir Melwas of the Summer Country, and is being held captive in his castle with many wounded knights. She bids you, for the love of God, to rescue them with all speed.'

Pausing only to arm himself, Lancelot rode for many hours. In the forest he was attacked by archers in Melwas' livery. They raised their bows and aimed into the belly of Lancelot's horse. He leapt to the ground and turned to avenge it. But the archers had already melted back into the trees, leaving Lancelot, his horse dead, and he himself encumbered with spear, sword and shield, to find his way on foot.

Before long he met a carter gathering wood. 'Good fellow, take me to the castle of Melwas and you shall be well rewarded.' 'I cannot do that. Sir Melwas sent me to gather wood, nor would he thank me for fetching his enemy, I think, since you speak of him so darkly.'

Lancelot held his sword to the man's neck. 'Nevertheless, you will drive me to the gate.' And he hauled himself and his harness into the muddy cart. ▷

HARNESS: ARMOUR

5th May

*G*uinevere and her ladies, weary with attending to the hurts of her knights, sat in the window of their prison-bower. They were trapped within an impregnable castle, on a small island surrounded by turbulent waters, with no hope of knowing whether the page had escaped with news of their abduction.

Lancelot rides in a cart to the rescue of Guinevere. His squire turns away his head in horror at this, for only condemned murderers rode thus.

Then one lady, whose eyes were sharper than the rest, espied the cart approaching on the opposite bank. 'Look, my lady,' she said, 'I suppose that poor knight in the cart is going to his hanging. If only he were free to rescue us!' Guinevere sharpened her eyes and looked more closely. 'Foul-mouthed wench! It is Sir Lancelot. As for the manner of his coming, clearly his horse has been slain. God keep him from so wretched a fate as hanging – such a noble knight to humble himself so for our sakes.' ▷

6ᵗʰ May

Lancelot's troubles were not yet ended. He saw how strong were the castle's defences and that the drawbridge was raised. 'How do you gain entry, fellow?' he demanded of the carter. 'There is a way – one that Sir Melwas himself uses – but you'll not want to try that unless you have the patronage of some saint or magician.' 'Show me,' said Lancelot. And the carter showed him where a bridge stretched from shore to castle – but so narrow that even a mountain goat would have found it difficult to cross. 'They call it the Sword-Bridge,' the carter said; 'It's the only way into the Summer Country.'

Guinevere and her ladies, leaning from their windows, gaped to see Lancelot go upon all fours, with his sword and shield strapped to his back, and inch his way across the perilous bridge, finding that as long as he kept his mind upon the rescue of Guinevere the bridge stayed firm, but that if his mind strayed, so it began to sway as though it had been a piece of rope. He gained the further shore at last. Surveying the castle, he saw a frightened porter peering round a gate to

In order to release Guinevere from the castle of Melwas, Lancelot has first to cross the Sword-Bridge, then fight two lions, and finally overcome Melwas' knights. Guinevere and her captor watch from the battlements.

72

assess his progress. Before he had time to withdraw, Lancelot charged forward, throwing the door back so that the breath was knocked from the fellow's body. Then, standing at last within the castle, Lancelot called his challenge: 'Melwas, false traitor and sometime knight of the Round Table, come forth and fight. I, Lancelot du Lac, challenge you.' ▷

7th May

Melwas' plot to kill Lancelot secretly had failed. Now he must face the greatest knight in the world alone. Melwas' craven heart knocked loudly in his chest. 'I will not fight you,' he cried at last. 'I will tie one hand behind me,' shouted Lancelot, 'And I will unarm myself upon one side. Then will you fight?' That Melwas could not refuse, and so it was done. With a cry Melwas rushed out and attacked Lancelot with ferocious speed. Lancelot spun away from the attack, drew his sword and with a single terrible blow cut Melwas' head open, so that the two halves fell apart like an apple cut with a knife. Then he went inside to release the Queen and her knights and ladies.

8th May

Sir Gawain, Sir Morholt and Sir Owain rode together in search of adventure. They came at last to the forest of Arroy, where it was said that no one who entered came away without meeting a wonder of some kind. And so they came to a deep valley full of stones, and there was a fountain, and sitting by it were three damsels. One seemed to be of sixty years, the second of thirty, the third of fifteen years, and all wore garlands of flowers about their brows. 'Ladies,' said Sir Gawain, 'why are you here?' 'To lead such knights as yourselves to adventure,' replied the eldest. 'And since you are three knights and we three damsels, you should each choose one to ride with you.' And Owain, who was the youngest, chose the oldest damsel, and Morholt took the damsel of thirty years, which pleased Sir Gawain greatly, because that left him the youngest of the three. And so the knights set forth in different directions, having agreed that they would meet again a year hence. ▷

9th May

Sir Gawain rode north. His damsel led him to a crossroads: there he met a solitary knight, with whom he broke a friendly spear. As the knight prepared to ride on, eight others appeared who all challenged him. With amazing ease he defeated them all one by one as Gawain watched in admiration. Then,

Owain, Gawain and Morholt set out on their adventures. They each meet and ride with a damsel, who leads them into strange and mysterious places.

surprisingly, the knight stood unmoving as the eight he had defeated surrounded and bound him fast, then carried him off. 'Will you not help this man?' demanded Gawain's lady. 'Nay, for this is not my quarrel,' replied Gawain. Then the lady began to insult him, calling him coward, and when two more knights rode up and challenged Gawain, while he was engaged in fighting one, the damsel went off with the other.

Gawain soon overcame the knight he had challenged, and was invited to stay at his castle. From him Gawain learned the story of the knight who had allowed himself to be taken prisoner. His name was Pelleas, and he loved a great lady named Ettard, who despised him. And because of this, although every day he fought with her knights, and overcame them all, he afterwards allowed himself to be taken to her castle so that he might catch a forlorn glimpse of her. 'Alas, this is a great pity,' said Gawain. 'On the morrow I will seek him out and do what I can to help him.'

▷

10th May

Next day Gawain met Pelleas in the forest and persuaded him to abandon his present course of action, in the understanding that Gawain would woo the lady on his behalf. Then, to attract her attention, Gawain took Pelleas' armour, and riding up to her castle claimed to have slain her would-be suitor. Ettard looked with favour on Gawain at once, and the two spent a day and night in dalliance, setting up a silken pavilion in the forest. There Pelleas found them in bed together, and such was his anguish that he almost slew them as they lay. But in the end all he did was to lay his naked sword by their heads, and then he rode away sorrowing.

▷

11th May

When they awoke and saw the sword Ettard was angered at the trick Gawain had played upon her, while he himself was smitten with remorse. 'We owe him an explanation at the least,' he said, and rode in pursuit. But in the forest Pelleas met with the lady Nimue, she who was to entrap Merlin himself, and when she divined the cause of his sorrow she cast a spell upon him that he should hate Ettard forever; and upon Ettard she cast a spell that she should love Pelleas. And thus, when they met, Ettard begged Pelleas to forgive her and take her as his own, but he had eyes only for Nimue and spurned Ettard coldly. Gawain, seeing the harm he had done so lightly, rode away in shame, while the lady Ettard returned to her home and died of grief. Pelleas resided with Nimue in happiness until he forgot Ettard completely.

▷

12th May

*S*ir Morholt and his lady rode south all day, but there was no sign of a place to stay the night. Then they encountered a man and asked if he knew of one. 'Aye, I know of a castle nearby, but I think you may regret its hospitality.' 'Nonetheless, we shall chance it,' answered Morholt, and they followed the directions until they came to the castle and were welcomed. Then, when its lord, who was the Duke of the South Marches, heard that Morholt was of the Table Round, his manner changed. 'This night you shall have lodging, but on the morrow you shall meet with myself and my six sons at once, for Sir Gawain slew my other son, and I have sworn vengeance on all Round Table knights.' ▷

13th May

*I*n the morning Morholt met with the Duke and his six sons, and there was a terrible mêlée. But he overcame them all at last and made them swear to offer fealty to King Arthur. Morholt and his lady rode on until they met other knights going to a tournament. There Morholt carried the day, and was required by the Lord Fergus, who had been at the jousts, to aid him with a dreadful giant whom none could overcome. And Sir Morholt agreed and overcame the giant after a long fight in a river; he was richly rewarded. Afterwards he went on to more adventures with his lady, until the year was up and it was time to meet his fellows again. ▷

14th May

*S*ir Owain rode east with his lady, and she led him, as she had promised, into many adventures of arms in which he proved himself a worthy knight. At the end she brought him to the Lady of the Rock, who had been deprived of her lands by Sir Hew the Red and his brother Sir Edward. Owain declared that he would speak with them about this, and went to their castle, where they had so many knights that the lady would not permit Owain by any means to attack them. But he did speak with Sir Hew and Sir Edward and they agreed to fight him, two against one, if he dared. Next day they met and the battle went on a long time, until the earth was stained red with all their blood, and the Lady of the Rock despaired for the life of Owain. But in the end, after a great struggle, he defeated both the wicked knights, who promised to return the lady's lands to her and to offer their fealty to Arthur. For the rest of the year Owain was nursed back to health by the Lady until it was time for him to meet with his fellows. The three knights returned to the fountain and met to recount their adventures, and only Gawain's lady had little good to say of him.

15th May

King Pellinore of the Isles rode in search of the lady and the knight who had carried her off by force. He met first with a maiden nursing a wounded knight in her arms. 'Help me, for the love of God!' But he ignored her pleading, so hot was he on his quest, and that maiden in her despair ended her own life on her lover's sword. In a clearing, he found Nimue, the maiden he sought, but she was being competed for by Sir Meliot and Sir Hontzlake. Sir Meliot had seen his cousin being abducted against her will and was attempting to defend her. Pellinore helped slay Hontzlake; then, riding back with Nimue, he came upon the bodies of the maiden and the knight. They had been eaten by beasts, all save the maiden's head, which he bore sorrowfully back to court. There Merlin told him that the dead maiden was none other than Eleine, Pellinore's own daughter, whereat the King was grieved beyond measure. It was in this wise that Nimue, the daughter of Dionas, was brought to court.

16th May

The time came when the child engendered upon Queen Morgause of Orkney by her half-brother King Arthur was to be born. And she gave birth to a strong dark-haired son whom she named Mordred. Arthur, knowing when the birth was due though not the day, gave out a terrible edict: that all children born on or about that day were to be taken and placed in a boat and set adrift – for he feared the prophecy of Merlin and the sin he had committed when he lay unknowingly with one of his own blood.

All was done as King Arthur commanded. A ship with five hundred new-born children was set adrift upon the tide. And it chanced that the ship foundered on the rocky coastline of northern Britain. All were lost save one, the child Mordred. He was washed ashore near a fishing village, and one of the fishermen discovered him and brought him home. But in time Morgause learned by her dark magic that her child was not slain, and recovered him. Thereafter she taught him to hate his father and began plotting Arthur's downfall.

When Merlin heard of the King's dreadful deed he groaned aloud, for now he knew that the doom of the kingdom was certain.

17th May

Sir Palomides the Saracen had loved Isolt of Ireland so long in secret that he grew desperate. Then one day as he wandered in the forest he met an old man who said: 'Palomides, there is a quest which awaits you.' And Palomides asked him what it was. At that moment there came a crashing in the bushes and a

From the moment he arrived at Arthur's court, Palomides the Saracen Knight was the centre of quarrel and disagreement. Here he is seen, on the left, fighting Tristan and Lamorack, who falls to the earth. A rival for the love of Isolt, Palomides later follows the Questing Beast, shown here in the background.

strange and terrible beast came forth: footed like a hart, with the body of a leopard and the tail of a lion, it had the head of a serpent and the noise of thirty couple of hounds coming from within it. 'This is the Beast Glatisant, of which you have heard,' said the old man. 'But that is Pellinore's quest.' 'No longer, for he is

slain by Sir Gawain and his brothers in revenge against the death of their father King Lot. Now this quest is thine, for this you may have, but not Isolt.' And Palomides turned in anger upon the old man, but he was gone from sight.   ▷

18th May

Thereafter Palomides pursued the Beast doggedly, and though he often turned aside for other adventures, yet he followed his quest. Many years afterwards, he caught the Beast, following it through the forest day and night without pause until his horse fell beneath him, and the Beast was too exhausted to go further. Then it turned at bay and Palomides struck it in the belly with his sword. It fell as though dead, but from its belly came out thirty couple of grisly hounds, that made to attack Palomides but turned aside when they scented water. He watched them drink until they were full beyond measure, and drink still more, until they burst, one by one. Then Palomides fell into a sleep, and when he awoke the Beast was gone, but in its place stood an old woman. 'I was the Beast, Sir Palomides, and long have I lived with the curse of my mother's sin. Now I ask that you take me where I may be shriven and give up my life.' And, full of wonder, Palomides found a hermit to whose care he gave the woman. And when she had confessed her sins she died. Thus was the end of the Questing Beast. But Palomides found no rest, for he loved Isolt as much as ever, and as ever was parted from her.

19th May

The wedding of Arthur and Guinevere was the most splendid occasion that had been seen in Britain for many years. Nothing like it could be remembered by any man or woman then living, and all knew that it ushered in a new era of peace and prosperity. The Fellowship of the Round Table was established, and already beginning to clear the land of evil.   ▷ 10TH JUNE

20th May

Arthur heard of a fierce boar that ravaged the country thereabouts. He swore to take the creature himself and rode forth accompanied by Sir Gawain, Sir Kay and Sir Baldwin of Brittany. When they had been on their way some time they heard the crashing of the great boar in the bushes and Arthur swore that he would capture it by the next morning. Then he bade the others swear oaths of their own: Gawain swore that he would wait by the haunted Tarn Watheling all night; Kay that he would patrol the woods in search of adventure; Baldwin that he would never doubt the truth of his lady as long as he lived.   ▷

SHRIVEN: CONFESSED AND GIVEN THE LAST RITES

21st May

Arthur pursued the great boar deep into the forest, where it turned at bay. After a mighty struggle, in which the beast's massive tusks at times came close to dealing him a terrible wound, he overcame it at last, skinned and cut it up with his own knife and carried it back to the court. ▷

22nd May

Sir Kay set out at once and in the forest he met a knight who rode with a damsel. When she saw Kay she begged him to save her from the knight. He, naming himself Sir Meneleaf, protested that he had won the lady in a fair fight, but still Kay came on. Meneleaf quickly unhorsed him and took him prisoner. Then Kay said that his companion was close at hand who would ransom him at once and the three rode on together to where Gawain waited by the Tarn. When he knew the story Gawain jousted with Meneleaf twice, once for Kay and once for the girl, and both times he overthrew the other knight. Thus was Kay ransomed and the girl released. ▷

23rd May

Arthur, Kay and Gawain sat together and discussed the vow of Sir Baldwin. 'I think we must put this to the test,' said Arthur, and gathering a party of knights he rode to Baldwin's castle and was made welcome for the night. They spoke nothing of their adventures but Arthur found a pretext to send Baldwin out for the night. Once he was gone the King knocked on the door of the chamber where Baldwin's wife lay abed, and demanded entry. At first she protested, but then opened in the King's name. Arthur, smiling, reassured her that she was in no danger, then commanded Gawain to undress and get into bed next to her. Then he called for lights and himself sat up playing chess by the bedside all night with Sir Kay. ▷

24th May

In the morning Baldwin returned and Arthur told him that he had found Gawain in bed with his wife and had remained there to keep watch. Baldwin merely smiled and said that he knew well that his lady was honourable – 'as is Sir Gawain' – and that there must be an explanation. The King and the rest began to laugh at that and Arthur clapped the knight on the back. 'You have kept your oath indeed,' he said, 'Be sure you will always have a place at the Round Table after this.'

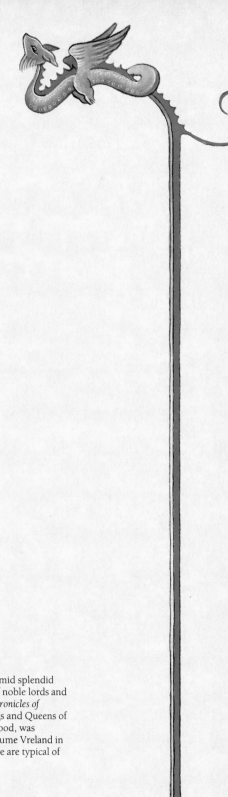

Arthur and Guinevere are married amid splendid surroundings and in the presence of noble lords and ladies. This illustration, from the *Chronicles of Hainault*, a great pageant of the Kings and Queens of Burgundy prepared for Philip the Good, was illuminated by the celebrated Guillaume Vreland in 1468. The costumes and architecture are typical of the fifteenth century. (19th May)

25th May

Disillusioned with life at Arthur's court and no longer able to return to Cornwall without disguise, Tristan wandered far in foreign lands, pursuing the trade of a mercenary knight. After many fruitless battles he came to Brittany, to the court of his cousin King Hoel, and there found employment in a local war between the King and one of his neighbours. Here Tristan found a friend in the person of the King's son Kaherdin, with whom he fought side by side to great effect. And, when the fighting was done and they returned to the Breton court, Kaherdin did his best to persuade Tristan to marry his sister, who happened also to be called Isolt. Though she looked not at all like Isolt of Ireland yet the name drew Tristan, and like a man still adrift in a rudderless ship he found himself marrying her, more for the friendship he felt for her brother than out of any affection he felt for the lady herself.   ▷ 18TH JUNE

26th May

Lancelot could not long abide at the court once the King had married Guinevere. For though he had been made the Queen's Champion, bound at all times to protect her from whatever danger might arise to threaten her, to see her daily was a pain to him that might not be borne. And so he requested and got leave to ride at errantry – a course which he was to pursue many times in the years that followed.

His first great quest led him into nearly every part of the kingdom, and he found no shortage of wrongs to right. Not all his experiences were straightforward, however. One day, weary from a long ride, he came upon a rich pavilion set up in a grassy field, and determined to ask for shelter. But when he looked within he found no one, and when he looked upon the bed that was made up with silken sheets, he yearned so greatly to lie upon it that he took off his armour and lay down with no thought as to his right to do so.

In the middle of the night he was woken by a man climbing into the bed beside him, who when he became aware of Lancelot's presence leapt up with a cry and snatched out his sword. Lancelot, still fuddled from sleep, acted instinctively. Drawing his own weapon, he struck out with all his great strength. The man lay bleeding before either had time to think what they were about. Next moment the man's wife entered the pavilion and began screaming. For a while confusion reigned, but eventually the truth was established. Lancelot begged forgiveness and rode to the nearest hermitage to bring a healer to the knight he had accidentally wounded. In after years the man became a staunch knight of the Round Table and both he and Lancelot could remember with a smile their first encounter.

27th May

On this day was King Arthur crowned in splendour and might in the City of the Legions. Kings and nobles from every part of the land came to do him homage, and there was a great tournament at which the sons of King Lot of Orkney – Gawain, Gaheries and Agravain – outshone all others in the field of combat. Many beautiful women attended the jousting, whose presence spurred the knights to even greater feats of strength and chivalry.   ▷ 3RD SEPTEMBER

28th May

Long after Gawain had unspelled Ragnall and married her he came again into contact with her brother Gromer Somer Jour – though he did not at first know that it was he. It came about that while the knights were sitting at table one day a squat, dark-featured Turk entered the hall, swaggered over to Gawain and almost felled him with a blow on the ear. Others leapt to hold the Turk, but he threw them off and said: 'Gawain, if you are not too afraid, I would have you accompany me on a journey.' Faced with this challenge Gawain could not refuse. He donned his armour and rode out of Camelot behind the Turk.   ▷

CITY OF THE LEGIONS:
CAERLEON-ON-USK

Here Arthur receives the crown of Britain seated beneath a canopy and surrounded by nobles. Outside, a spectacular tournament takes place in the meadows.

29th May

They rode for most of the day through the forest, then the Turk suddenly pulled his horse off the road and headed straight for a low line of hills to the north. As they approached, the hillsides opened and they passed within, both Gawain and his mount shying at the prospect of the dim world beyond. But all was light as day, though of the sun there was no sign. Presently they sighted a castle. 'Now,' said the Turk, 'enter if you dare. I shall be with you, but only you will be able to see me.' Gawain entered the frowning gates and found himself immediately surrounded by a gang of ugly giants, some more than eight feet tall. Concealing any fear he felt, he entered the main hall and there saw an even bigger, rougher fellow, sitting on a throne before a vast brazier filled with glowing coals. The giant leader, seeing Gawain, showed all his broken teeth in a laugh. 'Come in, little man, show us what you are made of.' He indicated that Gawain should lift the brazier. Clearly this was a feat beyond any normal man, but the Turk leapt forward, seized it in his arms and flung it at the giant. He fell back roaring with pain and surprise and the rest of the crew attacked Gawain. ▷

30th May

The next few minutes were fast and furious. Gawain laid about him with his sword, cleaving arms and legs and heads. The Turk picked up bodies and flung them against the walls where they crashed, slid and lay groaning. Then it was over, the fight won, and the Turk approached Gawain carrying a golden basin and a sharp sword. 'Now cut off my head and catch the blood in here.' Gawain protested but in the end did as he was bid. As blood spurted from the severed neck the figure of the Turk shimmered and shook and in his place stood a handsome knight. 'Sir Gawain,' he said, 'I give you thanks that you have set me free from the enchantment that held me. I am Gromer, Ragnall's brother.' Thus it came about that Gawain freed both brother and sister; thus also he learned that they were of the Otherworld, and that just as Gromer must now journey on thither, so his sister, lost to Gawain for long years, had gone before him. But Gawain must return to the land of men, or else remain in the Otherworld forever.

31st May

The Pentecost court gathered at Camelot and all went into the great Minster church to hear High Mass. When they came out they made their way to the Hall of the Round Table, where they found that on the back of the Siege Perilous, in letters of gold, was written: ON THIS DAY SHALL THIS CHAIR BE OCCUPIED. Then they all knew that great deeds were about to happen. ▷ 1ST JUNE

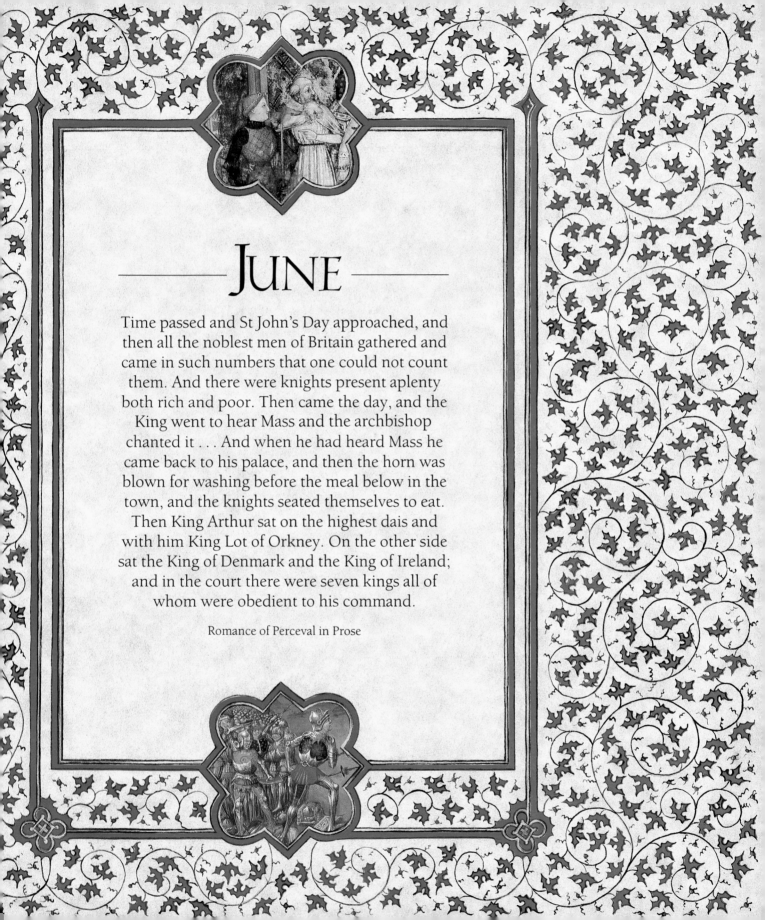

June

Time passed and St John's Day approached, and
then all the noblest men of Britain gathered and
came in such numbers that one could not count
them. And there were knights present aplenty
both rich and poor. Then came the day, and the
King went to hear Mass and the archbishop
chanted it . . . And when he had heard Mass he
came back to his palace, and then the horn was
blown for washing before the meal below in the
town, and the knights seated themselves to eat.
Then King Arthur sat on the highest dais and
with him King Lot of Orkney. On the other side
sat the King of Denmark and the King of Ireland;
and in the court there were seven kings all of
whom were obedient to his command.

Romance of Perceval in Prose

de samit qi parout sor ses espaules. a par
de dint estoit toies dun blanc samit.

Vant il la uestu et apareillie se li dit. ue
nes. aps moi sire. chr. et il li fist et il le
mene tot droit au siege pilleus de le. en
lane. se seoir. et leue le drae dont il estoit
couers qe lanc. ia uoit este metre se troue
les lettres qi disoient. a est li sieges galahu.

I pintremens regarde les lettres se tro
troue ci estoit le nom: se lour i hastes
er tcr leens sont. Sire. chr. asses uos
au. ci li seez tot seure.
mant. a uie aproume. Si uoz uos em po
et als. qe bien aues fet ce qe len uos co
manta. a salues moi tc: ces a tcz cele
tcl saint ostel. a mon auci le roi pilleu:

et mon bel auoel le roi resqueor. et li dites
de par moi qe tel li un dieou au pluz tost
qe ge pore et qe ge en aurai loisir.

Tant se pint li puinces. de leenz. a coina
de a teu nre seigneur. le roi a toute sa y
pignie. et qnt il constrent de madre. qil
estoit. sine tant onqes plet auuz. auui le
ur respont tot plenemant. qil ne lor dur
rci. pur au il le sauoier bien en cor tot a
aiuz. sil lisesoit remanter. Si uuer au me
stre deuz deu paiz. qi dont estoit si le o
uir. a teleno dual le chigres. illa corn a
troue. chia. qelle fust dire qe tut leduu
roient. et escriete ma deu tel. qil noir
de cort en tiel meniere qil ne sorti dir
de sor este. a uile force.

1st June

Next morning, as the Fellowship were on their way to the great hall, they espied a wonder. Floating downstream on the river came a block of rose-red marble, through which was stuck a sword. And upon it were written these words: NEVER SHALL MAN TAKE ME HENCE, SAVE HE BY WHOSE SIDE I SHOULD HANG. AND HE SHALL BE THE BEST KNIGHT IN THE WORLD. When King Arthur heard of this he came down to the edge of the river, and with him were Sir Lancelot and Sir Gawain. 'Now should you both attempt this marvel,' he said. But though both the great knights tried, and others after them, none might move the sword at all. The Fellowship went into the hall, and when they were seated there came in an ancient man and a youth dressed in red armour. And the youth said to the company: 'Peace be with you, fair Lords.' Then the old man led him up to the Siege Perilous and addressing the company said: 'I am Titurel, of the lineage of Joseph of Arimathea. I bring hither this knight, who is of the blood of kings, and through whom shall be achieved many great mysteries.' As the court watched in amazement, the youth seated himself in the chair where none but the long-prophesied hero of the Grail might sit. Then the old man said: 'In the river nearby there floats a sword. It is meant for this youth.' So the whole court made their way back to the river, and there the young knight easily drew forth the sword. The old man led him to Sir Lancelot and said: 'You have already given this youth the estate of knighthood. Now arm him with this sword.' Only then did Lancelot recognize the youth from the abbey. Gravely he placed the sword in the empty scabbard which hung at the young man's side. Then said the old man: 'Sir Lancelot, greet now your son Sir Galahad; son, greet your father.' At that Lancelot knew that this was indeed the child of Helayne the Grail Maiden, and he wept. But the Queen, where she stood, looked harshly upon the scene, which was witness to her lover's betrayal. ▷

2nd June

All the Fellowship returned to the great hall, and Galahad seated himself once again in the Siege Perilous, which all saw now bore his name. Of the old man there was no sign, but suddenly all the window shutters closed with a crash and there came a great crying of wind and cracking of thunder, and the day grew suddenly dark. Into the hall came a ray of sunlight, and within it floated an object covered in white samite. From it light shone, subdued but promising hidden glories. Then every man looked upon his fellows and saw them as never before, indeed as they truly were. A wonderful savour as of roses and spices wafted through the hall, and every man there had the food he most desired set before him – though whether it was spiritual food or true viands is not told. And so the

As the Knights of the Round Table sit down to eat, an ancient hermit enters leading a youth clad in red armour. This is Galahad, who is destined to sit in the Siege Perilous (shown here with canopy).

VIANDS: FOOD

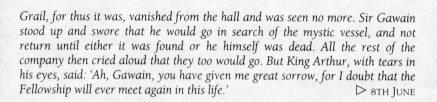

Grail, for thus it was, vanished from the hall and was seen no more. Sir Gawain stood up and swore that he would go in search of the mystic vessel, and not return until either it was found or he himself was dead. All the rest of the company then cried aloud that they too would go. But King Arthur, with tears in his eyes, said: 'Ah, Gawain, you have given me great sorrow, for I doubt that the Fellowship will ever meet again in this life.'

▷ 8TH JUNE

─────────── 3rd June ───────────

One day, while he was out hunting alone, Arthur lay down to rest by a fountain. There, as he lay between waking and sleeping, he thought he heard a sound like thirty couple of hounds in full cry, and there came past at a great rate the strangest beast that he ever saw. Though he knew it not, it was the Questing Beast. Soon after came a knight on a great horse, who paused by the fountain and asked of Arthur whether he had seen such a creature. Upon hearing that he had, the knight would have ridden at once in pursuit, but the king stayed him awhile and asked to know more of the beast. 'Sire, I am King Pellinore, that ruled sometime in the land of Gore. But this last year gone I have been unable to rest unless I follow this Beast, of which I have dreamed for long nights together. I know not how, but it seems that its fate and mine are bound together. For my brother King Pelles had also dreamed of the Beast. All I know is that I must follow it, until I either capture it or fall dead in the act.' So saying he mounted his horse and rode away again in pursuit of the Beast.

─────────── 4th June ───────────

As the court sat down to eat, there rode into the hall a beautiful maiden upon a mule with no bridle. 'Good King, grant leave to one of your champions to aid me retrieve the bridle. To the one who is successful, I will grant many kisses and more besides.' Many knights looked eager at this, for she was very fair to look upon, with full red lips ripe for kissing, but Arthur turned to his foster-brother, Kay, and granted the adventure to him. 'All you have to do is go where the mule leads you,' said the maiden.   ▷

─────────── 5th June ───────────

Perhaps it was the way that Kay rode the mule, or perhaps it was just in the nature of mules to dislike knights, but Kay passed some sorry adventures in search of the bridle. He had a poor seat on the sway-backed animal, and his feet dangled in the mire, which did not help his temper. The mule bore him through a

forest infested with lions and tigers, then through a valley of serpents. But though Kay was in some dread, none of these harmed him, out of respect for the mule's mistress. Lastly it bore him to a stream which had only an iron bar as a bridge: taking one look at its narrow, slippery footing, he was too afraid to cross, so he returned to Camelot.   ▷

─────────── 6th June ───────────

Gawain then took up the quest for the bridle. He passed the same adventures as Kay and crossed the iron bar bridge successfully, though the whirling gate of the castle on the opposite bank cut off half the mule's tail. Within the castle all was quiet, but Gawain was to find out why. The place was guarded by two lions, two serpents and a knight. He overcame them in turn in order to win the bridle, which was given him by the sister of the maiden whose mule he rode.   ▷

─────────── 7th June ───────────

Gawain returned to court with the bridle and gave it to the maiden. 'I have overcome the terrors of the castle and I am come to claim my reward,' he said, kneeling to her. The maiden raised him and showered him with kisses, so that all the other knights sighed in envious anticipation. But the maiden snatched up the bridle and mounted the mule: 'Kisses for the bridle bravely captured, Sir Gawain, but, as for the rest, I fear my promise can only partially be fulfilled, for you return my mule with only half a tail. I bid the court farewell.' And with that she rode out, leaving Gawain ruefully rubbing his chin in regret.

─────────── 8th June ───────────

Every member of the Round Table Fellowship who was fit enough to travel prepared to set out on the Quest for the Grail. They attended Mass in the morning and then assembled in the great square before the minster. There King Arthur addressed them, with tears in his eyes: 'You are setting forth on the greatest of all adventures. I fear greatly that we shall not all meet again in this life, but I wish you well and the protection of God and His Holy Mother.' The King turned away, weeping openly, and the archbishop blessed them all, one hundred and fifty, that were to depart. And they all swore upon the Holy Book to find the Grail or die in the attempt. The first to leave were Gawain and Lancelot, whose parting from the Queen had been a bitter one. As they rode through the streets of Camelot, there was great weeping upon all sides, for many knew they would not see the like of that Fellowship again.   ▷ 15TH DECEMBER

In this Italian manuscript the
Knights of the Round Table swear
to follow the Quest for the Holy
Grail. Arthur watches sadly,
knowing that many will not return.
(8th June)

THRENODY: LAMENT

9th June

*S*ir Lancelot lived on for another five months as a hermit, acquiring a
reputation of great holiness. But one morning he failed to rise, and when his
brother, Sir Ector de Maris, went to wake him he found that Lancelot was dead.
Ector made a great threnody over him, who had in his time been the greatest
knight of all the Round Table Fellowship. Then he journeyed to the Archbishop of
Canterbury, and the prelate came and read the words for the great dead over
him. It is said that Ector dreamed that night, and in his vision he saw Sir
Lancelot's soul carried to heaven by angels – though whether this is true or not no
man may say.

10th June

*T*he young King sat on his carved throne in the hall of his capital of Camelot,
and his beautiful young Queen sat next to him. Thirty lesser kings came to
pay their homage and one hundred and twenty knights sat down at the great
Round Table that day. Such a magnificent feast was not seen again for many
years, and all those who attended recalled it ever after as a most solemn and
joyous occasion.

▷ 26TH MAY

11ᵗʰ June

As was often the way, the Fellowship of the Round Table were restless, awaiting an adventure before they could eat. Finally a young squire named Gismirante offered to go looking for one. He had scarcely been on the road an hour before he encountered a beautiful Fay, who greeted him, and said that she knew his errand and was determined to help him. 'Take this,' she said, 'and return to King Arthur.' And she handed him a golden hair. 'The maiden to whom this belongs will make as good an adventure as any you could wish for.' And with that she vanished. ▷

12ᵗʰ June

Gismirante returned to court in great excitement. 'Let the feast begin,' he cried, and showed Arthur the hair. 'Make me a knight,' begged Gismirante, 'for this is surely my adventure.' Arthur agreed and the young man set forth at once. He wandered for weeks in the forest, then one morning he awoke to find the Fay staring down at him. 'You are not going about this in the right way,' she said. 'Let me tell you now that this hair belongs to a lady who lives not far from here. Every week she attends Mass in the church of St Martin, and in that time every person in the city has to stay inside. To come out and see her is to court death.' And once again she vanished. ▷

13ᵗʰ June

With this information Gismirante found his way to the city and, when Sunday came, hid himself in the church and awaited her arrival. Shortly there came in the most beautiful maiden he had ever seen, with whom he fell at once in love. She was guarded by two strange beasts, a lion and a griffin, who when they saw Gismirante would have attacked him, but the lady held them back. 'You should not be here,' she said, but not unkindly, for if the truth be known she liked the look of Gismirante almost as much as he liked her. Then she laughed and said: 'I want to escape from here – if you wish to help me be beneath the window of the westernmost tower in the city at midnight.' ▷

14ᵗʰ June

And so it fell out. Gismirante waited as he had been told. The lady appeared, looked down and said: 'How shall I carry all my jewels?' Gismirante said: 'You need bring none for my sake, I care for nothing but you.' With a smile the lady climbed down from the tower, disguised as a page, and the two fled the city.

A few hours later, they heard the thunder of hoofs – it was the lord of the city riding in pursuit. Gismirante turned at bay, but the lady drew out a wand with which she touched the road and at once there sprang up a thick forest. The sound of pursuit died away. Then the lady laughed and said: 'Be not amazed. I am the sister of the Fay who brought this adventure to you. Now that I am set free I would have you for my lover.' And Gismirante remained many months in her company, before he returned to Camelot to begin a knightly career of note.

15th June

Lancelot found it ever harder to ride in tournament or joust as his fame grew. He took to riding incognito, with a borrowed shield or helm, so that none might recognize him. One time he was at the castle of Sir Bernard of Astolat, who knew him not by sight, and of this good old man he asked to borrow his son's shield, who had been wounded and could not go to the forthcoming tournament. Sir Bernard had also a daughter, named Elaine, a maid of but fifteen, who, when she looked upon Sir Lancelot, loved him at once unto very death. And she begged him to carry her sleeve in the tournament, a thing which Lancelot had never done. Because he truly wanted to be in disguise, he agreed, and thus brought tragedy upon them both. ▷

16th June

At the tournament Lancelot cut a swathe through all the knights, both young and old. Many, including Sir Gawain, thought they recognized the style of fighting, but could not believe that it was Lancelot who carried a maiden's favour. Then in the last bout of jousting, by chance Lancelot's mount put a foot wrong; his opponent's spear slid under his shield and wounded him deeply in the side. With blood welling forth Lancelot fled the field, lest his disguise be discovered. He rode as best he might to Astolat and fell in a faint at the feet of Elaine. ▷

17th June

For the next weeks Elaine of Astolat nursed the great knight back to health. In that time her love for him grew stronger, though she never spoke of it until he was almost mended. Then one day, as she sat at his bedside, she ventured to look into his face and to utter the words she had been longing to say. Lancelot, the colour coming and going in his cheeks, told her that he was sworn to love but one lady. And after that he made ready to depart as soon as he might, for he saw in Elaine's face how deep was her hurt. ▷ 12TH NOVEMBER

A fifteenth-century depiction of the battle of Badon
(possibly Bath), in which Arthur finally breaks the power of
the Saxon invaders. Here he is shown in personal combat
with the Saxon leader Hengist. (19th June)

93

18th June

Tristan's marriage to Isolt White-Hands was a loveless one which both soon came to regret. On their wedding night Tristan turned from his bride, complaining of an old wound, and thereafter he avoided the marriage bed without pretence of desiring otherwise. On a day when Tristan, Kaherdin and Isolt rode out in the bright sun of high summer, as they crossed a small river, some water splashed up onto Isolt's leg. 'Ah,' she said wistfully, 'Would that you, my husband, were as bold as that water.' From this Kaherdin knew what he had already guessed, that the marriage was unconsummated and that Tristan bore little love for his sister of the beautiful white hands. From that moment his friendship with Tristan cooled.

▷ 7TH OCTOBER

19th June

On this day, say the Chroniclers, did King Arthur meet with the Saxons in battle at a place named Badon Hill, and there he made such a slaughter of them that never again did they attempt to overwhelm the land of Britain while Arthur lived. Thus the evil done by Vortigern was set right; thus was Arthur's fame bruited abroad until there was not a man in the whole of the western world that had not heard his name or knew something of the deeds of him and his knights.

It is told also that at this battle Arthur carried on his shoulder a shield bearing an icon of the Blessed Virgin, and that ever after he had an especial duty towards her who had protected him.

While on the Grail Quest Bors is faced with the question of whether to rescue his brother or a damsel in distress. He chooses the latter, and is here shown riding with the lady whom he has rescued.

20th June

Bors rode long and hard on the Quest. One day he was near a deep part of the forest when he saw suddenly through the trees a sight which filled him with horror. His own brother, Sir Lional, was tied naked to the back of a horse, while a man rode behind him striking him again and again with a thorn twig. Blood ran down profusely from a hundred small wounds, and Lional's head lolled sickeningly. Then, as Bors was about to go to his aid, he heard a cry and looking the other way saw a damsel being carried off by a huge knight. Bors hesitated only a moment before following the damsel. He overtook the big knight swiftly, challenged him, and fought him to his knees. Then he set off, with the damsel behind him, to find Lional. When he arrived at an abbey he found his brother there, resting after being rescued by Lancelot. Lional was at first savage with anger towards his brother for not coming to his rescue at once, but in the end the brothers were reconciled.

21st June

*O*ne day Arthur and Merlin rode out together, delighting in the warmth of the summer sun. They came by a fountain, where an armed knight sat by the road. 'Ho,' said he to the travellers, 'you may not pass.' At this Arthur became so furious that he challenged the knight, even though Merlin warned him of his prowess. The two fought for a long time, then at a crucial moment Arthur's sword, that which he had drawn from the stone and anvil, broke, and he would certainly have fallen had not Merlin, with a gesture, put the knight to sleep. Then Arthur bemoaned the breaking of his sword, to which Merlin replied, 'Never fear, a better one shall be yours.' He led him to a nearby lake, where stood a tall silver-haired woman. Merlin greeted her, saying: 'The King requires a fitting sword.' The woman silently raised her hand and pointed to the centre of the lake, where suddenly a hand holding a sword cleft the waters. 'Go now, and take your sword,' said Merlin. Arthur saw a little boat, and he went aboard it and poled it out to where the hand still held the sword. And he took it, feeling greater strength than ever before enter him in that moment. Arthur looked at the sword, which was encased in a sheath of plain leather, and drew it forth, whereupon it flashed with the fire of a thousand candles. Letters were engraven upon it which spelled the name EXCALIBUR. 'This now is your sword,' said Merlin. 'And while you wield it no man may overcome you. But the scabbard is even more valuable, for while you wear that you cannot be wounded.'

▷ 20TH APRIL

22nd June

*T*he King of the Western Isles had not paid any dues for so long that King Arthur decided to send Sir Gawain to find out why. He elected to take along with him Hunbaut, a grave and serious knight of whom little was known, though his bravery and trustworthiness were in no doubt. The first night they spent at the castle of a lord who guarded his daughter with greatest care, though she was already in love with Gawain. That night she found her way to his chamber, where they made love. In the morning the knights had to flee. Hunbaut reproached Gawain with his unknightly conduct, but the irrepressible knight only answered that the lady had sought him out for herself. ▷

23rd June

*N*ext night, the companions stayed at a castle where their host's daughter also desired Sir Gawain; but her father was jealous and protective. Next morning Gawain and Hunbaut were again forced to flee for their lives. They travelled to where they were to cross the sea to the Western Isles. There they

encountered a knight and were challenged to a duel. Hunbaut, who seemed to know the fellow, persuaded him to let them pass, and they sailed across to the main island. There they found the city oddly quiet. A man with a wooden leg challenged their entry to the castle, but Gawain pushed him into the moat.

A portrait of Gawain. Uncharacteristically he bears a lion on his shield, rather than the five-pointed star which was his best-known device.

Within the castle they met a fierce dwarf, who attacked Gawain so viciously that the latter was forced to slay him. They made their way into the great hall, where the King of the Isles sat sunk in meditation. Several times Gawain addressed him, without response, and Hunbaut now warned that they should leave, for he deemed that others of the court must soon discover their presence and attack them. Not without reluctance Gawain agreed to withdraw. The two soon found themselves pursued, but they successfully beat off an attack and gained the boat, which took them swiftly to shore again. There they encountered a damsel who wept bitterly because her father and lover had been captured by robbers and taken off in different directions. Gawain and Hunbaut agreed to separate and rescue both. ▷

24ᵗʰ June

Hunbaut successfully rescued the father of the damsel and returned to court, but there was no sign of Gawain. Hunbaut and several others set out in search of him. They found that he had been overwhelmed by superior numbers and thrown into prison. Hunbaut discovered that the robbers were in the service of the Lady of Gant Destoit, who loved Gawain so much that she had engineered the whole episode in order to capture him. He offered single combat to the lady's champion, and having overcome him demanded the release of Gawain. Bitterly disappointed that her hero had refused her advances, she was, in the end, only too glad to set him free. On returning to court Gawain and Hunbaut made a full report on the matter of the King of the Western Isles, and Arthur sent a larger force to ensure that he paid his dues.

25ᵗʰ June

Guinevere arranged a private dinner for the best of the Fellowship, except Lancelot who was absent. Because she knew of Sir Gawain's liking for apples she purveyed a dish of these specially for him. But a knight named Sir Pinal, who hated Gawain for his part in the slaying of his kinsman Sir Lamorack, secretly poisoned them. The company sat down to dine. Many courses of succulent meats were served, followed by subtleties fashioned in the likeness of turreted castles and fields of battle. An Irish knight, Sir Patrice, honoured by his inclusion in this company, stretched out his hand and took an apple, falling dead after one bite. At once his cousin, Mador de la Porte, leapt up, and accused the Queen of murdering Sir Patrice. It was no use for Gawain to plead that it was he who loved fruit and that an enemy had clearly meant the apple for him. Mador went straight to Arthur and demanded that the Queen be arraigned. ▷

SUBTLETIES: SUGAR
CONFECTIONERY

26th June

Reluctantly Arthur declared that the matter should be decided in trial by combat. Knowing that the evidence against the Queen was black, he sent urgent messengers to seek out Lancelot, while at the same time Guinevere sought elsewhere for a champion. There had been so much talk about Guinevere and Lancelot that the Queen's popularity had waned; some even thought her capable of poisoning Sir Patrice. And so it was that few knights wished to take up her cause. At length she persuaded Sir Bors, the cousin of Sir Lancelot, to uphold her name, though he seemed ill at ease with the idea. But all were waiting for Lancelot to appear. ▷ 29TH JUNE

27th June

At the beginning of the foundation of the Round Table Fellowship there were many evil men and women in the land of Britain. Gradually they were sought out and either killed or banished. Two, however, continued to hold out: Sir Breuse Sans Pité and Sir Turquine. Both fell at high summer, Sir Breuse to the hand of Gareth of Orkney, who slew him after a mighty battle. ▷

28th June

The very next day Lancelot met and fought with Sir Turquine. And of all his foes this was the one who came nearest to making an end of him. For Turquine was a grim and terrible figure whom no other man had ever bested. The battle lasted three days, and at the end of it both men were sorely wounded and the grass in the forest clearing was slippery with their blood. But at last Lancelot slipped beneath the guard of his antagonist and struck one blow which cleft him from crown to navel. Thus died the last of those who had caused such outrage before Arthur's day.

29th June

At the last moment, as the hour dawned for the trial of Guinevere for the murder of Patrice, Lancelot came. Speaking to no one, not even Guinevere herself, he entered the lists, drew his sword, saluted the King and Queen, and reduced Sir Mador to ruin in a matter of minutes. He, babbling, declared the Queen innocent, and there were ragged cheers from all the knights who had come there. But Lancelot rode away again at once, leaving Gawain to uncover the real plot and to bring the villain to justice. Guinevere was silent and withdrawn after this, and many smiled to see her discomfited.

30th June

*T*ristan continued to teach Isolt to play the harp. Suspecting nothing, Mark smiled upon them fondly, until a cousin of his named Andret noticed how closely the two sat, and how Tristan's hand would often brush against Isolt's seemingly by chance. Then Mark took to watching them together, covertly, until one day he saw Isolt take up the harp and play, while Tristan laid his head in her lap and let the sun warm them both. Isolt bent above the harp, her long tresses falling forward against her lover's face, and Mark saw what others had seen for a long while, that these two were lovers. Then his anger knew no bounds and he set a trap for them. One night he scattered flour on the floor around Tristan's bed, and in the morning saw the prints of a woman's naked feet. Thus the trap was sprung. But because of the honour in which Tristan was held as the strongest knight in all Cornwall, and also because of his own cuckoldry, Mark dared not have him openly arraigned. So he had Tristan dragged before him, struck him in the face and banished him forever from the court.

▷ 18TH JULY

To disguise the fact that they are lovers Tristan has taught Isolt to play the harp. Here she plays to him, while Tristan lounges in full armour on the bed.

JULY

Came with the Queen, women fair; all wives
of the rich men that dwelt in the land . . . In
the church, in the south half, sate Arthur the
King himself; by the north side (Guinevere)
the Queen. There came before her four
chosen queens; each bare in the left hand a
jewel of red gold, and three snow-white
doves sate on their shoulders; who were the
four queens, wives of the kings who bare in
their hands the four swords of gold before
Arthur, noblest of kings . . . Songs were there
merry that lasted very long; I ween if it had
lasted seven years, the yet they would more.

Layamon: Brut

1st July

*P*erceval was travelling beside the ocean when he saw a ship approaching. In the bow stood a beautiful maiden who called out to him that she had news of the Quest. Gladly Perceval went aboard and found a wonderful feast set out inside a silken tent on the deck. He talked for a long while with the maiden, who told him much that had occurred to other knights on the Quest. And she made herself seem so pleasant that as she stroked his hand and leaned softly against him Perceval felt himself slipping into a dream. Then he saw the cross-shaped hilt of his sword, which caused him to awaken. He saw that the maiden was half-naked and very beautiful, and in desperation drew his sword and wounded himself deeply in the thigh. Pain fountained through him and he heard a cry. Darkness closed over him and when he awoke he found himself ashore again, with no sign of the ship or its perilously lovely occupant.   ▷ 16TH JANUARY

2nd July

*S*ir Gawain and Sir Morholt rode in search of adventure together. One day they found themselves approaching a tall rock which stood like an island in the heart of the forest. They could see movement on its summit and heard the sound of clear voices talking and singing together. When they stood at last at the foot of the rock they could see a number of women on the top, looking down at them. 'Ah,' said one, 'It is Sir Gawain and Sir Morholt, they who will die just before the ending of the Round Table Fellowship.' Astonished, Gawain demanded how they knew these things. 'We are sisters,' said another of the women, 'and one of our number had the misfortune to quarrel with Merlin. He set us here by enchantment, which we cannot break. But we are enabled to see all things from this place. Indeed, everything that is to happen in this land is known to us.' 'How may we come up and join you?' demanded Morholt, for he could see neither stair nor path to the top of the sheer rock. 'That is easily done, if you truly wish it,' another of the damsels answered with a smile, and in a moment the two knights found themselves standing on top of the rock. From there they could see the boundless leagues of the great forest, even perhaps the sunlight flashing on the towers of distant Camelot.   ▷

3rd July

*T*hey stayed for several days, learning much from the nine ladies on their rock. But when they desired to depart, they found that they were not to do so easily. In the end they were captive there nearly a year, and then only set free from this gentle captivity by the agency of Gareth of Orkney, who happened to

pass nearby. Learning of the presence of his comrades, he found the brother of the nine women living close by and threatened to kill him unless Gawain and Morholt were released. But ever after Gawain remembered the things he had learned, and knew the time of his death, though not its fashion, from that moment on.

4th July

When Lancelot had been engaged upon the Quest for the Grail for a long while he came to a crossroads where there was an old ruined chapel. Being weary, he lay down to rest under a tree. After a while, half sleeping and half waking, he thought he saw a wounded knight carried on a litter, and when he came to the place where the chapel had once stood he prayed aloud to be healed. Then Lancelot saw a strange procession: candles all alight, a cross and something else, covered in a white veil, that he thought he remembered from the house of King Pelles. But whoever carried them he saw not. When he tried to rise he was unable to, but was forced to watch as the sick knight touched the veiled thing, and was at once healed. Where the things that had been borne invisibly from the chapel went then Lancelot could not say, but he watched as the healed knight knelt and gave thanks. Then, when the man's squire began to arm him, he found that he had neither helmet nor sword. The knight looked to where Lancelot still lay, and showed that he had been aware of him all along, for he said: 'Who is that knight who cannot even get to his feet when he is in the presence of the Grail?' And the squire answered: 'That is Sir Lancelot, the greatest of the knights of the Round Table.' 'Then take his helm and sword, and his horse which is better than mine. For he is so steeped in sin that he has no need of them.' And though Lancelot struggled he could move neither hand nor foot, but was forced to watch as the squire took his sword and helm and gave them to the knight, who rode away on Lancelot's own horse. Then he woke fully, and the things were indeed gone, and a voice spoke to him saying that he was unworthy to seek the Grail because of his love for Queen Guinevere. ▷

5th July

Then Lancelot was cast down utterly. Taking the horse which had belonged to the sick knight, he rode wherever it would go in the forest until he found himself at the dwelling of a hermit. There he went in and confessed all his sins, which were a great weight upon him, and he admitted that the great deeds of arms he had done were for the sake of the Queen rather than for good itself, or even for King Arthur. The hermit heard all that he had to say, then gave his

judgement. 'Sir,' he said, 'I know of no knight that has been greater blessed than you. For you have done great evil in loving the Queen. Yet you have been given strength, and a fair face, and a straight body. And you have been given to sire the knight who will succeed in the Quest for the Grail where none other might do so. But I say this to you: go from here and sin no more. And continue to seek the Grail, for though your son Sir Galahad shall be the one to realize the mysteries in full, yet has your quest much to teach you. For you shall come yet once more into the presence of the Grail.' Then he gave Lancelot what penance he might and sent him on his way.

6th July

After the discovery of his parentage Gawain returned to Britain in search of fame, fortune and his true family. He soon found his way to Caerleon, where Arthur was holding court. As he approached the city he met a strange knight on the road and challenged him to combat. They fought furiously for several hours until finally Gawain overcame his adversary, who ruefully admitted that he was indeed Arthur the King, escaped for a few hours from the affairs of state. Gawain

at once laid his sword at the feet of the young King and gave his own story. In wonder, Arthur greeted him as nephew and returned with him to the court, where Lot of Orkney, but lately joined with Arthur after opposing him with the twelve rebel kings, met his long-lost son in some amazement. Gawain discovered that he now had two brothers, Gaheries and Agravain, but it was some time before he met either them or his mother Morgause. In later years, when events soured his easy nature somewhat, he was never as much a part of Morgause's plotting with her sister Morgain as were his brethren.

7th July

Ever since the discovery of the love between Morgause and Lamorack, which ended in the death of their mother, the three sons of Orkney had planned the death of Lamorack. Finally they brought about his shameful end, setting upon him in the forest like brigands and attacking him as one. Even while he defended himself from Gaheries and Agravain, Gawain came upon him from behind and so slew him treacherously. Thus ended the feud between the houses of Pellinore and Lot. King Arthur, when he heard of the deed, banished the three brothers from court for a year, and many said that they were no longer to be trusted.

8th July

One day there came to King Arthur's court a youth named Brunor le Noir. He wore a rich mail-coat which had many rents and holes in it, and when he asked for the gift of knighthood from the King's own hand, Sir Kay looked at the ill-shaped mail-coat and said: 'Your title shall be La Cote Male Taile', which is to say 'the misshapen coat'. But the young man looked at him calmly and said: 'This coat was my father's, and he was murdered while he wore it. These cuts and rents were caused by the swords of his enemies, and I shall wear it until they are all brought to book.' Then Arthur thought that he liked this answer, and the demeanour of the youth, and so he agreed to give him knighthood the next day. And Brunor asked that when he received the accolade he should be called by the name Kay had given him in jest. ▷

ACCOLADE: BLOW ON THE
SHOULDER SIGNIFYING
KNIGHTHOOD

9th July

Next day La Cote Male Taile was knighted, and that same morning came a damsel bearing a black shield emblazoned with a white hand, who asked for a knight to fulfil the adventure of the shield. And La Cote Male Taile sprang forward to offer himself for this quest, at which the damsel was less than pleased,

having hoped for a better or older knight. But Arthur granted his request and the young man rode out with the lady, who was called Maldissant because of her sharp tongue. All the way she rebuked him for his youth and inexperience, even though he soon proved himself an able knight.

Meanwhile Sir Lancelot happened to return to the court and, hearing of La Cote Male Taile and the damsel with the shield, exclaimed: 'Shame on you all, sirs, for allowing this to happen. I know of that lady. She has led many knights to their deaths through the adventure of that shield, which has an ill reputation and calls all men to attack its bearer. I myself will follow this young knight, and give him what aid I can.'

▷

10th July

La Cote Male Taile was already in trouble, having encountered a band of powerful knights, all related, who attacked him furiously and drove him into the courtyard of their castle. His back to the wall, he fought grimly until weakened so much by loss of blood that he was overcome and imprisoned. There he might have languished had not Maldissant, repenting of her former hard words, ridden off and met Sir Lancelot, who at once rode to the castle, overcame the knights and set La Cote Male Taile free. Upon discovering who he was Lancelot greeted him warmly, and told how he had himself slain the murderer of Sir Helance le Noir, Brunor's father, years before. Thus was the young man's quest fulfilled. He soon married the damsel of the shield, who was called Beauvivant after that, and Brunor took the castle where he had been imprisoned for his own. But ever after he was called La Cote Male Taile, even though he no longer wore the misshapen shirt of mail.

11th July

Lancelot continued to seek the Grail, and at last, after many adventures, he came to a castle which seemed deserted, save that it was defended by two lions. Lancelot slew them both without difficulty and entered the castle. He came to a door that would not open, and heard from within the sound of voices raised in glorious praise to God. He pressed harder upon the door, until it opened at last and he looked within. There he saw an altar at which an aged priest was celebrating Mass, but the vessel he used was no ordinary chalice – light flamed from it like that of a hundred candles. Also, though there seemed no other person there, the voices of a great choir could be heard, singing praises.

Awed, Lancelot stood looking in, and saw the priest raise the Host – only it was not a wafer, but rather the body of a Man bleeding from wounds in hands

and feet and side. When Lancelot saw the frail old man struggling to hold the body, he went forward to help. But a great light blasted out upon him the moment his foot crossed the threshold, and he fell down to the ground, blinded and nearly unconscious. He felt many hands lift and carry him outside and lay him down. In the morning the people of the castle returned and found him there; they laid him in a bed, where he remained for twenty days. ▷ 14TH SEPTEMBER

──────────── 12ᵗʰ July ────────────

*S*ir Tristan loved Isolt more than life itself, but there was another who loved her equally, though his passion was not returned. This was Sir Palomides, a Saracen knight who chose to fight upon the side of King Arthur and who became a knight of the Round Table through his strength. And though he found reason to be at the court of King Mark as often as he might, in order to get a view of Isolt, and though he wrote her songs of surpassing beauty in the Eastern mode, yet never did she once look upon him with anything but scorn – for which reason Palomides wandered far and wide in search of adventure in order that he might forget his unrequited love. ▷ 17TH MAY

──────── ◇ ────────

Tristan and Palomides the Saracen have become implacable rivals for the love of Isolt. Here they meet in the forest. Palomides (on the right), though he wears a suitably oriental hat, is shown as a European.

──────── ◇ ────────

13th July

Once Meraugis and Gorvains had been great companions-in-arms, but they fell out over the love of Lidoine, the daughter of King Cavalon. Lidoine submitted her case to Arthur in order to keep the peace. A special court of ladies arbitrated and decided that Meraugis should be allowed to pay court to Lidoine for one year and so prove himself worthy of her love. A dwarf reminded Arthur that Gawain had been absent for a long time on his quest for the Sword of Miracles, and Meraugis took this as his quest. Together the lovers set forth, for Lidoine accompanied her knight on his adventures. ▷

14th July

Meraugis was unable to find Gawain and so he rode to the place of Merlin's imprisonment to ask directions. Above that mysterious place, on top of their high rock, sat the nine sibyls, who gave him directions to a crossroads with three ways signposted. Meraugis took the one called 'the Nameless Road' and so came to the Nameless City where he and Lidoine were welcomed with joy. ▷

15th July

The people were glad to see Meraugis, because he was the one destined to fight the Knight of the Island. As he came into the field, Meraugis realized that this was none other than Gawain, who had been captured by the Lady of the Island, and who could not be released until he was overcome in combat. He and Meraugis had a mock duel, during which Meraugis feigned death. Then, that night, Meraugis put on female apparel and escaped with Gawain. ▷

16th July

Lidoine believed that Meraugis had been killed and fled to take refuge with a nobleman called Amice. On her way to her friend's manor, she was abducted by Belchis. Lidoine sent word to Gorvains to rescue her, believing him to be her only hope. Meanwhile, Meraugis had wandered into an enchanted garden and had been rescued by Belchis' own brother-in-law. Learning that they were under the same roof, the lovers rejoiced. But Gorvains soon arrived and Meraugis, out of jealousy of his old friend, fought on Belchis' side. To put a stop to this, Lidoine begged them both to return to Arthur's court and there fight a duel. Before the assembled knights, Meraugis and Gorvains fought it out until Meraugis triumphed. Gorvains relinquished his claims on Lidoine and she and Meraugis were married.

17th July

When Arthur was first chosen King of Britain through the test of the Sword, there were certain kings, twelve in all, who denied him. This led, inevitably, to war. For two long years the young King fought against the league of the twelve. Many deeds of new heroes were sung at that time. Finally a great battle was fought near the wood of Bedegraine. There, through the magic of Merlin and the warcraft of Arthur himself, the rebels were finally overthrown. Many were killed, including King Lot of Orkney, the most powerful of them all. Those who were still alive at the end of that fateful day swore allegiance to Arthur.

▷ 19TH JULY

18th July

Only once did the two greatest knights of Arthur's time fight together. Lancelot, acclaimed by all the Best Knight in the World, and Tristan, wanderer and only rarely part of the Round Table Fellowship, met by chance at the Perron Stone, set there long since by Merlin to mark the tomb of Lanceor and Columb. There Merlin had prophesied that the two mightiest fighters and greatest lovers of their day would meet and fight, and so it was. Neither knew the other: they fought all morning and into the afternoon, till each could scarcely either hold a sword or remain on his feet. At last, with no sign of either knight's giving way to the other, both paused for breath and raised their visors, and when each knew who it was he fought they both offered their swords in surrender and sat and spoke long together.

Tristan's love for Isolt was by then well known, and, perhaps because of it, Lancelot spoke of his love for Guinevere. For never had he voiced to any man living the love which he bore for the Queen, since by such talk might she be besmirched. Thus began a friendship that was to last until death parted them, and the two great knights ever after avoided each other in tournaments, so none knows to this day which was truly the better.

▷ 25TH MAY

19th July

With the deaths of the twelve rebel kings there were no others to withstand Arthur. Merlin had made, in token of this, twelve statues, of lead and copper, gilded with gold, in the shapes of the twelve; and each one held a taper of wax that burned day and night. Over them all he set a statue of King Arthur with drawn sword. But to Arthur he said, sadly: 'While these tapers burn I shall be with you; but when they burn no longer I shall be gone. And after that shall come about the adventures of the Sangreal.'

SANGREAL: THE HOLY GRAIL

---------- 20th July ----------

*P*erceval was sojourning in the wildest regions of Arthur's kingdom. He came to a castle and begged a bed for the night. 'Better you go elsewhere,' said the lady of the place, 'for the nine witches of Gloucester are nearby and they devastate the countryside.' ▷

---------- 21st July ----------

*A*s midnight struck, the castle was assailed by great combat and Perceval rushed to assist in its defence. He saw a great woman slay the watchman and he levelled the back of her helmet with his sword. 'Mercy, good Perceval.' 'How do you know my name?' he cried. 'I am your destiny, for fate has woven us together. In the name of her whom you love in your heart and whom you saw figured in the bloody snow, I bid you go with me. For I shall arm you well and teach you another chivalry.' And Perceval went with the witch into the regions of the Otherworld and became accomplished in the use of magical arms.

---------- 22nd July ----------

*A*fter the Quest of the Grail was over the shattered remnants of the Round Table Fellowship gathered again at Camelot for a feast. As Arthur himself had long since supposed, there were many gaps in their ranks, with more than seventy of the knights either known to be killed or missing. Therefore Arthur sent fourth a message through the whole kingdom announcing a great tournament at the city of Lonazep, where every knight and lady who wished might watch the jousting, and where new knights would be found to fill the empty seats at the Round Table. ▷

---------- 23rd July ----------

*T*here came to the tournament of Lonazep every able-bodied knight in the kingdom. All the great fighters were there, Lancelot, Tristan, Palomides, Gawain, Gareth, and the rest, as well as many younger men, who sought fame and fortune against their elders. But of all those who shone at that long tournament none was more outstanding than the Saracen Palomides. For to this tournament here openly came Isolt of Ireland with Sir Tristan, and King Arthur himself said nothing, having learned of the evil way that King Mark had behaved towards them. Some said that by condoning the love of Tristan and Isolt he must therefore condone the love between his wife and Lancelot.

Palomides sought to shine in the eyes of his lady, though in truth she scarcely

At the Tournament of Lonazep, all the Round Table knights
left alive after the Quest for the Grail meet for one great
gathering. It is to be the last, for soon after the breaking of
the Fellowship takes place.

seemed aware of him. And this perhaps led him to extremes, for he struck down Tristan after he had been unhorsed, and without waiting for him to recover – a deed which earned him no honour despite his great feats. Tristan himself forgave his old rival, and the two fought each other to a standstill in the mêlée, when all the rest – even Lancelot, who had received a deep wound in the thigh – had fallen or retired. ▷

──────── 24th July ────────

At last, after the tournament was over, Palomides came before King Arthur and requested that he become a Christian, as both his brothers, Sir Sefere and Sir Segwarides, had before him. And many there rejoiced to see him baptized, and even Isolt of Ireland smiled upon him, for which reason he and Tristan became reconciled at last.

──────── 25th July ────────

A young knight named Gauriel of Muntabel once set out to visit the court of the famed King Arthur. On the way he entered a region where he saw no men at all, only many lovely women. One of them, Fluer, he dared to love, but on learning of his presence in her lands – for she was a Queen – she laid upon him an enchantment which made him hideously ugly to all who beheld him. Then she summoned Gauriel before her and, mocking his ugliness, told him that he would be restored only if he could bring to her land three of the greatest of the Round Table knights. ▷

──────── 26th July ────────

Gauriel set forth on his errand and soon arrived at Arthur's encampment near Carlisle. A damsel came forth to meet him, and he took her captive – though treating her well – until such time as Arthur's knights could challenge him and win her back. ▷

──────── 27th July ────────

Several tried, but Gauriel defeated them all. Then Gawain, Owain and Erec returned from a long adventure and each went out to encounter the powerful young knight. He succeeded in unhorsing all three, but was then overcome by Gawain. Admitting the reason for his actions, Gauriel persuaded them to accompany him to the land of Fluer. ▷

28th July

As they approached they found a large army of knights assaulting the home of Gauriel's love. The four attacked from behind and put the whole force to flight. Having thus proved himself, Gauriel was commanded to take a bath, and the ugly appearance was washed off in the water. He then married the Queen and became a faithful vassal of Arthur's for the rest of his days.

29th July

With Isolt of Ireland lost to him again, Tristan crossed the sea to Brittany. There he chanced to receive a wound while out hunting. The wound, which was a deep one, became poisoned, so that he sickened and lay close to death. Then he took off the ring that Isolt had given him long ago and gave it to a messenger to take to Ireland, begging Isolt to come and heal him. And he said to the man: 'I shall watch for your return. If Isolt is with you, show a white sail, if not let it be black.' ▷

Tristan, wounded to death in Brittany, raises his sword in a last gesture of strength, while his wife Isolt of Brittany and her brother Kaherdin look on. This is the final frame of a three-frame strip; the whole picture is shown overleaf.

30th July

As his condition worsened, Tristan became too weak to rise from his bed even to watch for the returning ship. Isolt White-Hands nursed him gently, and in the weeks of his illness they drew closer than they had ever been. But Isolt knew of the message sent to Ireland, and a bitterness grew in her against her namesake. So, when at last the ship was sighted, though it bore a white sail, yet when Tristan weakly asked the colour, Isolt told him it was black. When he heard this Tristan turned his face to the wall and gave up his slender hold on life. Thus when Isolt of Ireland stepped ashore he was already dead, and when she saw him such was her grief that her own heart broke, and she stretched herself out beside him and died. Many people mourned the death of the lovers, even those who had condemned them in life. They were buried together in a single grave at the behest of Lancelot, who came to mourn his friend at the last.

And as for Isolt of the White Hands, she could not bear the reproaches of those who knew the story, nor could she contemplate life without Tristan, and she went to the cliffs near her father's castle and threw herself down, so that her body was lost forever in the endless sea.

31st July

Vortigern fled to Wales to avoid the invading Saxons and the wrath of his own people. His counsellors bade him raise a high tower near Yr Wyddfa, as a place of safe retreat. Masons set to work but, whenever they laid the foundations, they were swallowed up by the next day. Vortigern's Druids said that the tower could never be raised unless the blood of a boy who had no father was shed on the foundations. Accordingly, Vortigern sent messengers through the land to discover such a child.

▷ 1ST NOVEMBER

Top: Tristan continues playing the harp to Isolt even though wounded by an arrow. Centre: King Mark and an accomplice carrying a poisoned dart intended for Tristan (in one version of the story). Bottom: Tristan's death, seen in more detail on p.113.

AUGUST

For ever, said Arthur, it is a worshipful knight's
deed to help another worshipful knight when he
seeth him in a great danger; for ever a worshipful
man will be loath to a worshipful man shamed;
and he that is of no worship and fareth with
cowardice, never shall he show gentleness, nor
no manner of goodness where he seeth a man in
any danger, for then ever will a coward show no
mercy; and always a good man will do ever to
another man as he would be done to himself. So
then there were great feasts unto kings and
dukes, and revel, game, and play, and all
manner of noblesse was used; and he that was
courteous, true, and faithful, to his friend was
that time cherished.

Malory: Le Morte DArthur

1st August

Nimue, the daughter of Dionas, was a maiden of great skill, having the blessing of Diana and the wisdom of the Lady of the Lake's realm within her. The combination of her beauty and otherworldly skills drew the love of Merlin, who knew no maiden of his own kind. Merlin taught her many wondrous things, for she was an insatiable student of enchantment. Her only desire was to learn Merlin's deep wisdom, yet he was sparing of his study and busy in affairs of state. One day she asked how to make a tower without wall and Merlin, unthinking, taught her. While he lay sleeping, Nimue made a circle of her wimple about him and, walking nine times about it, raised up a tower of glass. When he awoke, he protested: 'Sweet love, why have you done this?' Nimue smiled, 'Now you will do my bidding and teach me all you know, for you cannot leave here unless I will it.' 'That will never be,' said Merlin, 'for I will not teach you any more, lest you wreak enchantment upon the kingdom.' And so it was that Merlin remained a prisoner in the glass castle. And though Nimue frequently entered to entreat his tutoring, Merlin ever refused her.
▷ 6TH AUGUST

Merlin, lovesick for Nimue, shows her magical visions, including this one of two lovers playing and singing to each other.

2nd August

Gawain, Kay and Bishop Baldwin rode to the hunt. As night fell they were far from Camelot and bad weather set in. 'Where can we rest this night?' asked Kay. 'I know a place nearby,' replied the Bishop, 'though I fear it is a rough place and its lord, the Carl of Carlisle, an even rougher man.' 'Let us go there anyway,' said the others, and they rode swiftly until they came to a dark and frowning fortress. The Carl came out to meet them, a huge, ugly man with a twisted lip and broken nose. But he made them welcome civilly enough, and when they entered the hall there was a blazing fire. However, lying around the fire were four huge beasts: a lion, a bear, a bristled boar and a gigantic bull. As the three men drew back the Carl roared at the beasts in a thunderous voice, and they slunk away, snarling or snorting after their kind.

The weather was growing rapidly worse, and first Sir Kay and then the Bishop went outside to see to their horses. When the Carl returned alone Gawain began to fear for the lives of his companions. So he too excused himself and went to the stables. There he found both Kay and the Bishop stretched out on the straw, groaning, while a foal stood shivering in the doorway. Gawain at once threw his cloak over the beast, then went to see to his friends. Both had been knocked out but were otherwise unhurt. Hearing a footstep behind him Gawain turned to see the Carl. 'Had your friends been as good to my horse as you, Sir Knight, instead of driving it away so their own mounts could feed, they would not now be lying there,' and he turned and strode back into the hall. ▷

3rd August

By the time Gawain had revived his companions and they had all returned to the hall, supper was ready. The Carl's wife joined them: a beautiful woman whom Sir Kay at once engaged in conversation. After a while the Carl leaned across the table and said: 'You had better forget what you are thinking, sir, or you will surely have cause to regret it.' Kay flushed crimson and fell silent.

As supper was ending a beautiful girl entered with a harp and began to play most skilfully. Then it was time to retire for the night and the Carl himself showed the three travellers to their rooms. Gawain was last of all, and when he entered the chamber he found the Carl's wife waiting. 'Now,' said the Carl, 'I wish you to kiss my lady – but do nothing more, or it will be the worse for you.' So Gawain did as he was bid, not without being roused to passion, for the lady was fair indeed. 'Enough,' growled the Carl, and waved his wife away. Then the girl who had played for them entered. 'This is my daughter. She is yours for this night,' said the Carl, and departed. Gawain looked at the lovely girl and she at him, then he took her in his arms and carried her to the bed. ▷

4th August

Next morning the three knights met in the hall for breakfast. The Carl entered after them and sat silent until they were done. Then he took a great old spear from the wall and handed it to Gawain. 'Throw this at me,' he said. 'Do not fear, you cannot harm me.' So Gawain took the spear and flung it with all his might at the Carl, who ducked so that the spear shattered against the wall. Then the Carl came forward and embraced Gawain. With tears in his eyes he led them outside to the back of the hall. There he showed them a cart full of human bones. 'All these men I killed,' he said, 'because not one of them passed the tests I set them – to do whatever I asked without question. Only you, Sir Gawain, have succeeded. I am freed of my vow.' Bishop Baldwin crossed himself, and both the knights looked askance at the grisly remains. 'Sir,' said Gawain, 'I think we should all return to King Arthur's hall and let him decide this matter.' ▷

5th August

The Carl came willingly enough, and his wife and daughter accompanied them. Arthur heard the story in silence, then said: 'You have done great evil, Sir Carl, but the judgement must be God's. Now that I have your word that you will do no more harm in my kingdom I pardon you.' The Carl rejoiced, and confessed then that he had been compelled to do what he had done by the arts of the sorceress Morgain le Fay. Then all looked more kindly upon him, while the Carl turned to Gawain and offered him the hand of his daughter. Gawain was glad to accept, for he had a great liking for the girl. And she made him happy indeed until she died bearing a son, who was named Guingamore.

6th August

It had been many months since Arthur had seen Merlin and he sent Gawain to search for him. Gawain rode in the forest of Broceliande and it seemed that he heard an unseen voice. He came to the place of the glass tower, where Merlin instructed him in all that had befallen. 'Greet well the King and Queen, and tell them how it is with me.' And Gawain made much sorrow, for he had heard the cry of Merlin and had been unable to liberate him. ▷ 29TH DECEMBER

7th August

Gawain was a long while recovering from wounds he had received in battle, but one morning he felt strong enough to ride forth to take the air. He saw a silken pavilion set up, and coming from it as fair a maiden as he ever saw.

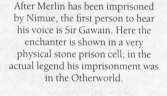

After Merlin has been imprisoned by Nimue, the first person to hear his voice is Sir Gawain. Here the enchanter is shown in a very physical stone prison cell; in the actual legend his imprisonment was in the Otherworld.

Merrily she welcomed him, and as he took off his helm and the sunlight struck his face she gasped aloud: 'You are Sir Gawain!' she cried, 'You I love best of all men now living,' and she threw herself at his feet and kissed them. Then Sir Gawain raised her up gently and they went into the pavilion, where the knight took off his armour and passed the time in the sports of love. But when he at last took leave of the lady – not without tears – he found himself overtaken by a tall knight who named himself the maiden's brother, Bran de Lys, and demanded that Gawain fight him for her honour which he had despoiled.

At another time Gawain would perhaps have found it easy enough to defeat Bran, but the weakness he still felt from his wounds made the match uneven, and he was himself struck down and left for dead. He was discovered lying in his own blood; he was carried back and nursed once more to health.   ▷

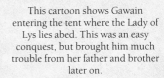

This cartoon shows Gawain entering the tent where the Lady of Lys lies abed. This was an easy conquest, but brought him much trouble from her father and brother later on.

8th August

A year almost to the day King Arthur, with some of his knights, including Gawain, were staying at a castle when Gawain suddenly caught sight of a shield on the wall. Rising from the table he took his sword and helm and sat with them to hand, refusing to eat. When questioned he confessed the story of the Lady of Lys, and said that the shield belonged to her brother. At that moment Bran himself entered and challenged Gawain to finish the fight. With Arthur and the rest looking on the two men began to battle furiously, neither giving way, until a damsel rushed forward with a child in her arms and cried upon them both to stop. The infant looked up at the bright swords, poised above him, and laughed

with delight. Then Arthur himself came forward and stopped the combat. Reluctantly the two men clasped hands and the damsel presented Gawain with his son. Afterwards Gawain married the Lady of Lys, though he left her, as was his way, after no more than five years, and she saw him no more.

————— 9th August —————

Perceval's dreams persisted, only now, instead of a great mourning, he kept dreaming of two women. One was as old as the earth and the other as fair as the stars. The first one rode upon a dragon and the second on a lion. The fair one bade him look to his quest for the Grail. She reminded him of the woman of his heart, for whom he remained ever chaste. The ugly one admonished him for his lack of speed and unfortunate behaviour. She was so like his tutor in arms that he woke sweating with embarrassment.   ▷ 2ND OCTOBER

————— 10th August —————

Almost a year to the day that the youth named by Sir Kay 'Beaumains' came to Camelot, a maiden appeared desiring succour for her mistress, who was being besieged by the terrible Red Knight of the Red Launds. At once Beaumains stepped forward and craved his second boon, that he be given this adventure. And because Arthur was a prince of his word he agreed, at which the maiden was angry indeed: she had asked for a great knight and had been given a 'kitchen knave'. But Beaumains followed her anyway, asking that Sir Lancelot should ride after them and give him knighthood. This Lancelot did, for he had grown to respect the youth in the past year.   ▷

————— 11th August —————

To Lancelot Beaumains confessed his true identity, and was knighted as Sir Gareth of Orkney, son of King Lot and youngest brother to Sir Gawain. Then he set off to follow the haughty lady, who, when he caught up with her, refused to address him as other than 'kitchen knave' and offered him constant insults – even when he rescued her from a band of robbers.   ▷

————— 12th August —————

On the second day of their journey Beaumains met and fought with the Knight of the Black Launds and took his armour. But still the lady, who was named Linet, spoke only insults to him.   ▷

A fifteenth-century illumination showing the arrival of Linet at Arthur's court. Sharp-tongued, she is ill-pleased by the King's decision to send the untried Gareth to help her besieged mistress.

LAUNDS: LANDS

13th August

On the third day Beaumains fought and defeated the Green Knight of the Green Launds, brother to the first knight he had overcome. But still Linet had no good word for him. ▷

14th August

On the fourth day Beaumains fought the Blue Knight of the Blue Launds, and now at last the lady Linet began to look more kindly upon him, though she still called him names and made a show of remaining downwind, 'away from the smell of grease'. On this same day they arrived at the castle of Linet's mistress, Lionors; Beaumains had a sight of her, leaning from her tower window, and at once he loved her as he had never loved any maiden or damsel in his life. ▷

15th August

On the fifth day Beaumains fought the Red Knight of the Red Launds, and a mighty fight it was, lasting all day until almost nightfall, when the young knight at last laid his adversary low with a great blow to the helm. And so the Red Knight, whose name was Sir Ironsides, gave his word to leave off besieging Lionors and to present himself to King Arthur for judgement. Linet could no longer refrain from praise, and when she knew the true identity of the 'kitchen knave' she was ashamed and spoke willingly to her mistress on Beaumains' behalf. Soon the two were wed; then all returned to Camelot amid general rejoicing and Gawain welcomed his brother while Sir Kay stood dumbfounded.

16th August

Lancelot came to Camelot as a king's son, and with a lineage that stretched back to Joseph of Arimathea himself. Imbued by the Lady of the Lake with magical strength, he soon proved himself the strongest knight ever to sit at the Round Table. He remained unbeaten from then until his death, save by one other, his son Galahad.

17th August

When Arthur first became High King of all Britain, the land of Lyonesse was ruled by a good lord named Meliodas. And in time his wife was due to bear him a child. But a few days before the birth King Meliodas vanished, tricked and imprisoned by a sorceress. The Queen, distressed almost out of her mind by this,

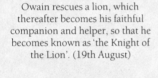

Owain rescues a lion, which thereafter becomes his faithful companion and helper, so that he becomes known as 'the Knight of the Lion'. (19th August)

rose from her bed and ran weeping into the forest, pursued by her ladies, who feared for her life. She fled until she could go no further, and then her time came upon her. And the child was great and her travail terrible, so that by the time her women found her she was almost unconscious, and becoming weaker and weaker. At last the child was born, a strong and sturdy boy. And his mother asked to be shown him, then said: 'Son, you have killed your mother.' To her ladies she said: 'If my lord is found remember me to him, and let him name our son Tristan.' Saying which the lady died, and was carried home. ▷

18th August

Merlin, meanwhile, had discovered Meliodas and released him. He returned to learn of his wife's death and was smitten with sorrow. But in time he came to love another and took her to be his new queen. She gave him sons also, and turned against Tristan, whom she saw as a threat to her own offspring. So great was her hatred that she attempted to poison him, though this was unsuccessful. When the king learned of her act he banished her and her children, and sent Tristan to Brittany to be brought up by a trusted knight named Governal.   ▷ 25TH APRIL

19th August

Owain wandered in his madness, growing steadily less like a man and more like a beast. He came upon a young mountain lion unable to leave its den because of a great serpent. Grown strong and cunning in the ways of beasts, Owain grappled with the serpent until it fell dead. The young lion came out and fawned before its rescuer and became his companion.   ▷

20th August

While Owain walked with his lion, he overheard a voice which seemed to issue from under the ground. He discovered an underground cave and a woman trapped inside. 'Who are you?' he asked, speaking the first words since madness came upon him. 'I am Luned and I am imprisoned here because it became known that the knight I rescued and married to my Lady of the Fountain was her husband's killer. They plan to burn me. If only that good knight was here for I love him best of all men.' Remembrance began to stir in Owain: 'What was his name?' 'Why, Owain, son of Uriens,' she replied. Owain's mind cleared. He waited until squires came to take Luned away and then set his lion upon them. As they fled, he released Luned and they escaped.   ▷ 19TH OCTOBER

21st August

Leodegraunce of Cameliarde was a faithful husband to his wife except on one occasion, and that brought about by magic. On the night that he engendered the child who was to be Guinevere, King Arthur's future queen, he was tricked by the magic of an evil sorceress into lying also with the wife of his chief huntsman. She too conceived a daughter, who was born at the same hour as Guinevere, and was her twin in every way save for a birthmark on her left thigh. She was named Genievre. As her likeness to Leodegraunce's daughter grew more marked, she was kept hidden from the eyes of the court, even her true father knowing nothing of her existence. When she was twelve years old, a damsel came from Morgain le Fay, who persuaded her parents to give the child into her care. From this time Genievre had but one purpose in life – to replace her half-sister as Queen of Britain when the time came. Morgain was assisted in this by a knight named Bertolait, who had been banished by Leodegraunce for the murder of another man. He in fact married Genievre, and the two were installed in a castle belonging to Morgain. One day Arthur was lured there, and given a potion through which Genievre convinced him that she was the true Guinevere and that her sister was a false creature sent by evil men wishing to control the King. Arthur believed her; he returned to court and, shockingly, ordered the Queen to be cast into prison. None knew the truth or could tell which of the two women was the real Guinevere. ▷

22nd August

A terrible period followed the imprisonment of Guinevere and her replacement by Genievre. Lancelot, as soon as he heard the news, returned to Camelot and, once he had visited the captive Queen, forced Sir Kay to give her into his custody. He took her at once to Joyous Gard where, for a brief time, they were happy. Arthur, angered at the presumption of his best knight, came close to sending an armed force to arrest them both, but good sense prevailed and he decided to leave well alone. ▷

23rd August

What might have happened had fate not taken a hand cannot be known; but one morning Arthur awoke to find Genievre stiff and speechless beside him. Her breathing was fast and shallow, her body rigid with silent agony. Arthur sent for doctors, who could do nothing. Finally a hermit named Amustans arrived at the court and gave Arthur a long lecture on his failure to perceive the truth. As the scales began to fall from his eyes Arthur sent for Leodegraunce and

his wife. Finally the huntsman and his wife were summoned and the whole matter brought into the open. Arthur, shamed by their confessions, recalled the true Guinevere, who, for the good of the land, returned to him as his Queen, despite her desire to remain with Lancelot. The false sister, still stupefied, was returned to the place where she had first tricked the King. There, Bertolait was found to be in a similar state, speechless and motionless. Later, recovering the power of speech and movement, they were both tried and burnt at the stake.

24ᵗʰ August

*G*ereint was happy with his wife, Enid. He had inherited his father's estates in Cornwall and now rarely performed feats of arms or even hunted much, so that his meinie complained. Enid noted this and mourned silently. One morning she woke and gazed upon her husband: 'How wretched I am to be the cause of his lack of honour.' The tears fell from her eyes upon Gereint's naked chest and he awoke. Dreaming and waking mingled in his understanding and he thought Enid to be weeping because she had been unfaithful. He bade her dress in her worst dress and ride after him. He also told her to be silent, whatever happened, for he meant to drag her about the countryside until she was properly shamed and fittingly punished.* ▷

MEINIE: HOUSEHOLD

25ᵗʰ August

*T*aking the worst roads and frequenting the wildest places, Gereint encountered many dangers. Several times, Enid noticed robbers or outlaw knights upon the road and warned Gereint, to his great anger. Several times, Gereint almost died from his stubborn combats with ferocious opponents, in defence of Enid, whom these men would have carried off and ravished. Arthur's*

Merlin and Vortigern stand by the pool in which the
red and white dragons do battle. Merlin points out
the meaning of this and delivers other prophecies
while Vortigern's Druids stand by, amazed.
(29th August)

126

court was encamped in the forest where they rode and many pitied Enid her bedraggled appearance and long-suffering silence; many begged Gereint to cease his shameful behaviour. But Gereint was determined to take on as many dangerous adventures as he could to show Enid his prowess. He accepted healing from Arthur's physician and then rode on his way. ▷

26th August

They came to Raven Castle, where Earl Owain lived. Everyone on the road warned Gereint not to go there, for all knights had to play a perilous game if they accepted hospitality from Owain, whose mother's kin were of otherworldly stock. This only made Gereint spur forward eagerly to embrace danger, while Enid trailed patiently behind. Owain greeted them warmly. After supper, he saw how Gereint was pale and withdrawn. 'Say but the word and you shall not have to enter the enchanted games,' he offered. Gereint compressed his lips. 'Show me what I have to do.' ▷

27th August

Owain showed him a high hedge with stakes about it. On each of the stakes was a man's head. Beyond the hedge was a mist and beyond the mist an orchard. Gereint went through it and found a tent with a golden chair in it, in which he seated himself. On an apple tree hung a hunting horn. A faery maiden of great beauty came and sat next to Gereint, warning him not to sit there. Soon Gereint was challenged by a faery knight and found himself fighting for his life. Drawing upon the patient love of Enid, Gereint struck his final blow, which unhorsed his opponent. 'I crave mercy! Speak, and I shall do your will!' 'I wish these games to cease for all time,' cried Gereint. The faery woman bade her companion blow the horn: 'Announce the joy to the world, that Gereint and Enid are no longer the prisoners of suspicion and misunderstanding. Seek now your lady's forgiveness and be as true to her as you have been strong in your deeds.' And this Gereint did. ▷

28th August

The faery knight had once been a mortal champion of great strength called Mabonagrain. He had served in the world of Faery for twenty years and now the blowing of the horn caused him to regain his mortality. He had entered the enchanted gardens as a young man; now he was past his prime. Gereint accordingly took him into his service and made him steward of his lands.

BOAR OF CORNWALL: KING
ARTHUR, ON WHOM THIS TITLE
WAS CONFERRED BY RIGHT OF
HIS MOTHER IGRAIN

29th August

Merlin listened to the story of his birth and challenged Vortigern's Druids: 'If you are so wise, tell me what lies under these ill-laid foundations.' The Druids bit their lips with ire and frustration, for they were ignorant of the tower's collapse. Merlin ordered a pit to be dug. 'Beneath this place you will find a pool and in it two hollow stones. There two dragons lie sleeping.' Such was Merlin's authority that Vortigern believed him. When the pool was drained, he descended to see for himself. It was as Merlin had said. A white and a red dragon were revealed and they began to fight ceaselessly. ▷

30th August

Vortigern asked: 'What do the dragons signify?' This question opened up the otherworldly well of prophecy within the young Merlin: 'Alas for the Red Dragon: its end is near. The people of Britain shall be overwhelmed by the White Dragon of the Saxons and all that is beautiful within this land shall be laid waste! Only the Boar of Cornwall shall defend it.' He prophesied the future of Britain until the ending of the world. Vortigern was subsequently surrounded by the rebellious British and burnt alive in his tower. ▷ 25TH FEBRUARY

31st August

Lancelot dreamed. An old man appeared to him and said: 'I am your grandfather. If you would attempt a great adventure go into the Perilous Forest and seek a fountain by a tomb which bleeds.' Waking, Lancelot set forth and searched until he found the place described in the dream. It was guarded by two lions. Lancelot slew them both but did not approach the tomb. Instead he looked into the fountain. The water bubbled and boiled and in it floated the head of the old man in his dream. Lancelot put his hand into the boiling water and withdrew the head. A voice called to him and, looking up, he saw an old ruined chapel. A hermit-like man beckoned. 'You have done well, my son. Now see if you can open the tomb.' Lancelot set his hands to the rim and lifted it easily. Within lay a headless body. Taking the head from the hermit he laid it reverently within. 'This is your grandfather's body,' the hermit said. 'He loved a good woman honourably. Others thought differently, and whispered to the husband. He had your grandfather murdered while he was drinking from this fountain. No one could remove the head because of the boiling water. In time another will come, the greatest knight of all. He will end this.' Lancelot and the hermit buried the body in the chapel. In time Galahad, Lancelot's son, came to the well and when he placed a hand within, it ceased boiling.

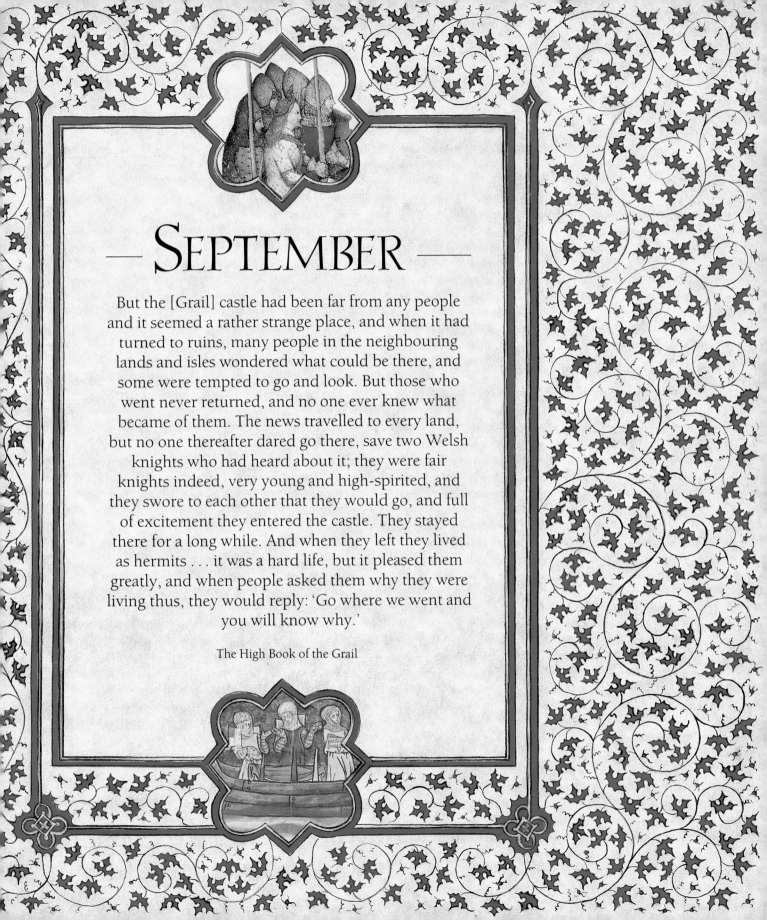

— SEPTEMBER —

But the [Grail] castle had been far from any people
and it seemed a rather strange place, and when it had
turned to ruins, many people in the neighbouring
lands and isles wondered what could be there, and
some were tempted to go and look. But those who
went never returned, and no one ever knew what
became of them. The news travelled to every land,
but no one thereafter dared go there, save two Welsh
knights who had heard about it; they were fair
knights indeed, very young and high-spirited, and
they swore to each other that they would go, and full
of excitement they entered the castle. They stayed
there for a long while. And when they left they lived
as hermits . . . it was a hard life, but it pleased them
greatly, and when people asked them why they were
living thus, they would reply: 'Go where we went and
you will know why.'

The High Book of the Grail

1ˢᵗ September

Four months of joy had Tristan and Isolt at Joyous Gard, but all the while Mark, once he learned of their escape from the lepers, plotted to entrap them. At length he sent a party of knights, led by the jealous Andret, to go by dead of night and steal Isolt away. Tristan himself was not there on that day, having received a message to attend a meeting of the Round Table. When he returned he found Isolt gone, and several of Lancelot's retainers dead. He returned angrily to Arthur's court and put his case before the King. Arthur confessed that there was little he could officially do: he might condone the lovers in private, but as King he must revile them and support Mark. He therefore did the only thing that he deemed possible – he sent a message to Mark commanding him to take back Isolt, to forgive her publicly, and to refrain from any further punishments. To this Mark reluctantly agreed, though inwardly he cursed the name of the King. Isolt was kept a virtual prisoner, while Tristan, in despair, went wandering.

▷ 29ᵀᴴ JULY

2ⁿᵈ September

Gawain had been engaged upon the Quest for the Grail for a long while when he came to the castle of Lady Fortune. He did not know at first that it was her castle, though it seemed the most wonderful place in the world, all encrusted with jewels

While Tristan is absent King Mark abducts Isolt from the castle of Joyous Gard where the lovers had found shelter.

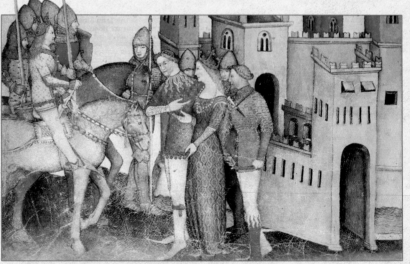

and rare stones. Gawain halted before the doors, which swung open, and he went within. There, in a vast hall, was Fortune's Wheel, and the Lady herself seated in a chair on top of it. And ever it seemed to spin, altering the fortune of those who sat upon it with every moment, now better, now worse. It seemed to Gawain as he looked at her that one half of her face was fair, and the other ugly. But as he looked, the wheel stopped, and the Lady became all beauty. 'Welcome, Gawain!' she cried. 'Long have I awaited your coming, for your fortunes have been at my disposal this long year, and many and oft times have they changed.' Gawain knew this only too well, and smiled ruefully. The Lady continued. 'It grieves me to say that you shall not achieve the Grail, but I have here for you a gift of great worth.' And she took off her own hand a ring that sparkled with sapphires and diamonds. 'He who wears this ring shall have the best that fortune can bring. I bid you take it to King Arthur, for so long as his kingdom is established he shall have good luck.' And afterwards, when the Quest was over, Gawain did indeed give the ring to Arthur. But later it was lost, and the King ever after had bad fortune. ▷ 20TH JUNE

3rd September

Among those who came to witness the coronation of Arthur as High King was the widow of Lot of Orkney, Queen Morgause. With her came three of her four strapping sons, Gawain, Gaheries and Agravain, who outshone all the other contenders in the great tournament arranged to celebrate the occasion. Arthur, being young and foolish, conceived a great love for this lady, although she was of mature years; she was passing fair, some said by virtue of her powers as a sorceress. So it came about that he bedded with her, and that a son was engendered upon her. But he knew not, though she was well aware of it, that she was his own half-sister, Morgause being a daughter of Igrain. Of this incest Mordred was conceived, he who was to be his father's doom, and Merlin saw what had occurred and knew there was naught he could do to avert what was to be, but he sorrowed greatly because of it. ▷ 6TH SEPTEMBER

4th September

There was once a knight named Caradoc, the son of Eliaures, who suffered a terrible affliction. A sorceress to whom he forbore to give his love had attached to his left arm a serpent which sucked at his blood and could not be removed. His greatest friend, Cador, and his betrothed love, Guimier, sought a way to relieve him of this scourge, but Caradoc fled to hide in the forest for fear of what his love would think of his emaciated body. ▷

5th September

After much searching Caradoc was found, living as a hermit, and a way was discovered to set him free. Two baths must be procured, one filled with milk, the other with wine; Caradoc must get into the bath of wine and Guimier into that of milk, then the maiden must expose her breast to the serpent so that it was drawn to transfer itself from Caradoc to her. In the space between the baths Cador must be ready to kill the creature. All went as planned: Guimier bravely allowed herself to become the target and Cador severed the serpent in twain with a single blow. Caradoc and his bride soon married, and he became a great knight of the Round Table. But because of his suffering his left arm was ever crooked, and thus he was known as Sir Caradoc Briefbrass, or Shrunken Arm.

6th September

One day Arthur rode hunting in the forest alone. It was not easy for him to escape the attentions of courtiers now that he was King. When he reached a certain fountain in the heart of the wood he tethered his horse and sat deep in thought. After a while he saw a young boy coming towards him. The youth addressed him boldly: 'King Arthur, I greet you and I know you well. I know who were your father and mother and all that you have done since you were King.' Angrily Arthur waved the youth away. 'How could you know any of these things, who are yet so much younger than I?' 'Nonetheless I know them,' said the youth as he departed.

Soon after there came an old man with white hair, who greeted the King and was made welcome. He said: 'Lord King, I greet you, and tell you that you have done an evil deed, though all unknowing. For you have lain with your half-sister Morgause, and you have begotten on her a son who will be your doom.' And Arthur bemoaned his fate and demanded to know how the old man could know these things. 'I am Merlin,' was the reply, 'and you knew me not when I came to you in the likeness of a child; therefore I took upon myself this likeness, and now you are wont to believe me. I grieve for your fate, yet it shall be better than mine, who shall be shut up by one less powerful than myself.' Then he was gone, leaving Arthur to wonder at the dark deed he had done. ▷ 16TH MAY

Merlin appears to Arthur first as a youth, then as an old man, and tells him of his future.

7th September

On his return to Britain from Ireland, Tristan learned that in his absence his uncle's barons had approached Mark with a request that he marry and give Cornwall an heir. Mark was at first reluctant. A bird then flew in through the window with a long strand of golden hair in its beak. It dropped this before Mark

and flew away, and the Lord of Cornwall declared that he would marry whomever the hair belonged to. Tristan, heartsick for Isolt, offered to lead the search for the owner of the hair. ▷

8th September

N̲ext day Tristan set forth, having no idea of where he should go, and realizing that Mark, for reasons of his own, did not intend a bride to be found for him. Tristan's road led him to the court of Arthur, where he was made welcome and quickly proved himself. Then one day, as he sat at table, a woman came into the hall and confronted him. 'You grow lax in your quest, sir knight,' she said. 'Tonight on the evening tide from the shore of this land sails a ship with no known destination. If you sail upon it you shall find what you seek.' Then she vanished away none knew where. So Tristan once again embarked on a ship that was to carry him to another encounter with his destiny. And often he took out the golden hair and looked upon it and wondered who was the maiden to whom it might belong. ▷ 20TH FEBRUARY

9th September

O̲ne day Lancelot came to the village of Corbin, and there he saw a fair tower with a strange glow about it. The villagers came forward to meet him, crying: 'Welcome, Sir Lancelot, for now we shall be set free.' And when Lancelot asked them what they meant, they replied that there was in the tower a damsel who had been kept imprisoned there a long time, and that until she was set free the whole village lay under a curse. So Lancelot entered the tower, and before his face all the bars and bolts opened. He came to a room at the top of the tower and there found the damsel, who sat in a bath of boiling water. When Lancelot took her hand she was able to step forth, naked as a needle, and he led her outside, where the villagers brought her clothes. Then they took Sir Lancelot to the nearby castle of Corbin, where the damsel's father came forth to greet them and there was much rejoicing. The damsel's father thanked Sir Lancelot fervently and told him that he was King Pelles, cousin to Joseph of Arimathea, and that his daughter's name was Helayne. Then he took Sir Lancelot inside and made him welcome. While they were at dinner there came into the hall the damsel who had been rescued, carrying an object covered in a white veil, that shone forth and filled the whole room with a sweet savour. And when Lancelot asked what this thing was King Pelles answered that it was the Grail itself, and that 'when it next appears in the realm of Arthur, it shall be the beginning of a great Quest that shall destroy the kingdom.' ▷

When Lancelot discovers the deception by which he has spent a night with Helayne of Corbin he comes close to slaying her. As it is, her confession that she is to bear his child drives him temporarily mad:

Learning of Lancelot's madness Guinevere sends knights forth to look for him. When he is discovered, her ladies hang around his neck a shield sent by the Lady of the Lake, which depicts Lancelot and the Queen. This brings him partially back to his senses, and in the last part of the picture the Lady of the Lake anoints her foster-son to make him sleep and awaken fully restored.

10th September

Now King Pelles knew from a prophecy made long since that if Sir Lancelot lay with his daughter he would beget upon her a knight of such prowess that he should win the Grail. Therefore he plotted how this might be brought about. There was a woman named Brisen, who was wise in the ways of potions and small magics. She had been Helayne's nurse and so was to be trusted. She it was who told Pelles how he might bring about the birth of the destined child: 'Lancelot loves only Queen Guinevere. Therefore let him believe that it is the Queen who calls him to her and he will do what must be done.' ▷

11th September

Next night Brisen contrived to have Lancelot drink some drugged wine, then, when he was all befuddled, she sent a man to his chamber with a ring that purported to come from Queen Guinevere, and with it a message that she awaited him at the nearby castle of Case. Lancelot at once got up and rode furiously to the castle, where he was admitted and shown to a room that was all darkened. In the dark a hand reached out for him, and because the drug had heated his blood Lancelot lay with the lady that he believed to be Guinevere. ▷

12th September

In the morning, Lancelot rose and opened the shutters. Thus he discovered that the lady in the bed was not Guinevere, but Helayne the daughter of King Pelles. Such were his anger and dismay that he drew his sword and would have slain her. But the girl threw herself at his feet, all naked, and said: 'Sir, be not angry with me. I did but the wishes of my father. And be assured, the child I shall bear shall be a great and worthy knight. I have it on the word of my good nurse

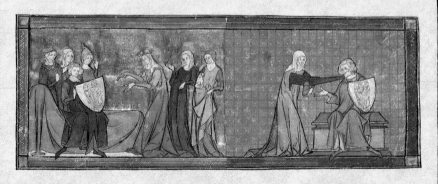

134

and of my father, who has long harboured the prophecy that of his line should spring a knight of surpassing holiness.' Lancelot let fall his sword and, giving a great cry, sprang out of the window, dressed only in his shirt, and fled into the forest, stark mad. There he remained for many months, until all believed him dead. But Guinevere sent knights to seek for him, and at last they found him, living on nuts and berries in the forest. His hair and beard were matted, and he had long ago replaced his shirt with the hide of an animal. He looked, in truth, like a wild beast. At first he would recognize no one, but at last Guinevere instructed one of her knights to show him a shield that had been made in the likeness of two lovers who resembled Lancelot and the Queen. When he saw that, Lancelot's eyes became clear, and he fell into a deep sleep. His cousin Sir Bors took him to Corbin, where Helayne nursed him back to health.

13th September

Owain followed Colgrevance's trail and soon came upon the King of the Animals, and so onwards to the fountain where he cast water upon the green stone. At once, there was thunder, lightning and rain and a great singing of birds, and the black knight appeared and fought Owain. They fought all day until Owain pierced his opponent's armour. The black knight was mortally wounded and turned for home. Owain gave chase even to the portcullis of the castle, which admitted its lord but which came down upon the back of Owain's horse and sliced it in two. Owain was in desperate straits, stuck between the portcullis and the inner gate, and in his enemy's hands. A maiden peered at him and thrust a jewelled ring through the lattice. 'Take this ring,' she said, 'wear it with the stone clasped in your hand and you will be invisible. When they come to arrest you, slip through and meet me by the horse-block within and I will hide you.' Owain put the ring on immediately and did as the maiden said.   ▷ 15TH SEPTEMBER

14th September

After many months of wandering Lancelot came to the shore of the sea and found there the Ship of Solomon awaiting him. Aboard was Galahad, alone, and thus the two men, father and son, spent days together in the peace of the ship, talking of many things: of the past, of their lives and feelings, of Galahad's task which, he had always known, must succeed but which also meant the ending of his life. And at last the time came for them to part, which was a gentle moment, not without tears upon both their cheeks. And Lancelot set out wandering again, with thoughtful mien, while Galahad sailed on to the place where he would meet Perceval and Bors.   ▷ 27TH SEPTEMBER

15th September

Owain had been hidden by the maiden Luned for two days. From his hiding-place in the tower he witnessed the funeral procession of the Knight of the Fountain and the rending grief of the knight's lady, who tore her hair and scratched her breast in a frenzy of mourning. As soon as the Lady of the Fountain returned from church, Luned went to work: 'My Lady, there is no one to defend this castle or to guard the fountain which belongs to you. Let me send to the court of King Arthur and find a new husband for you.' The lady screamed abuse at Luned at first, but soon saw the sense of her handmaiden's argument. ▷

16th September

Luned pretended to go away and come back the next day. 'I have found a worthy lord for your defence.' And she presented Owain, freshly accoutred in arms she had provided, in a mantle of yellow satin with the device of a lion upon it. And so it was that Owain put off his own device of the raven. The Lady of the Fountain accepted him as her husband and gave him the arms of the Knight of the Fountain, all of deepest black, and Owain defended the fountain from all comers. ▷ 17TH OCTOBER

17th September

When Galahad had journeyed far upon the Quest of the Grail he came to the shore of the sea and found there a mysterious ship awaiting him. On the side was written, in letters of gold, THOU WHO SHALL ENTER INTO THIS SHIP, BEWARE THOU BE STEADFAST. FOR IF THOU FAIL I SHALL NOT HELP THEE. And he went aboard and the ship sailed of its own accord to another place. ▷

18th September

And in that other place Galahad found Perceval and Bors awaiting him, for both had been told in dreams to go there. Each greeted other as old friends and comrades will, and learned of each other's adventures. ▷

19th September

Then the three knights went aboard the ship again, and there they found a great bed with a canopy made of three kinds of wood: one white, one green and one red. Attached thereto was a letter which told how Solomon the Wise and his Queen had learned of the great deeds that would be done by one of their line –

Lancelot greets his son Galahad as they prepare to go aboard the Ship of Solomon, which will carry Galahad to the Castle of the Grail, although his father will not be permitted to go with him. (14th September)

After many trials and tribulations
Owain finally marries the Lady of
the Fountain while her knights and
ladies look on. (16th September)

Galahad himself – and had prepared the ship to carry him, setting it adrift upon the seas of time. The bed was made of the wood of the Tree of Knowledge of Good and Evil, and the three kinds of wood that held the canopy were of the same. They were coloured thus because at the beginning the tree had been all white, but after the birth of Abel it became green, and after the murder of Abel it became red, betokening the colour of blood. And Galahad lay upon the bed and slept, and dreamed of the Grail. ▷

20ᵗʰ September

Also in the ship the three found a great sword in an ancient sheath. On it was written: LET HIM WHO SHALL DRAW ME OUT OF MY SHEATH BE MORE HARDY THAN ANY OTHER; AND WHO THAT DRAWETH ME, HE SHALL NEVER FAIL, OR BE WOUNDED TO THE DEATH. *And the knights read of how Solomon's Queen had taken the sword of King David, setting it with rich jewels, and that when she laid it on the ship, Solomon remarked on the humble hempen belt from which the sword hung, but his Queen prophesied it would be replaced by a worthier belt in time.* ▷

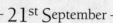

21st September

On the scabbard was written, on one side: HE THAT SHALL WIELD ME SHALL NEVER BE DEFEATED, AND THE BELT WITH WHICH I AM BELTED ON SHALL NOT BE CHANGED UNLESS IT BE BY A VIRGIN OF PUREST INTENT; and on the other: HE THAT SHALL PRAISE ME MOST SHALL FIND ME TO BLAME AT MOST NEED. ▷

22nd September

For a long while the ship sailed on until it touched land again. There they found waiting for them Perceval's sister Dindrane, who was a most holy maiden, brought up as a nun. And she came aboard the ship and told them the meaning of the things that had puzzled them. The meaning of the sword was that it should be borne by the greatest knight in the world, that is, Galahad himself, and if any other wore it it would fail him at the time of his greatest need. And the scabbard was to be belted upon him by a new belt, made not of the old material but of her own hair, which she had woven into a girdle of gold. ▷

23rd September

The three knights learned that in a distant time one of Galahad's own ancestors, a king named Lambors, had found the ship, had gone aboard and had tried to draw forth the sword. But it had turned in his hands and struck him through the thigh, so that he had become, like so many of the other kin to Joseph of Arimathea, wounded. ▷ 27TH SEPTEMBER

24th September

Gawain's son Gwigalois had many adventures, none more extraordinary than when he set out to rescue the husband of the lady Beleare. Her husband, Morel, had been stolen away by a dragon-like creature which lived beneath the Hollow Hills. Gwigalois found its lair, but no sign of Morel. Then the creature itself appeared, walking upright like a man but with massive clawed forefeet and a head which breathed out fire. Gwigalois had been gifted with a crystal spear and a flower of rare beauty. Now he held the flower before him like a shield and, as the beast recoiled, struck it to the heart with the spear, which melted to nothing as it took the life of the creature. But in falling the beast pinned Gwigalois under it, so that he fainted. When he recovered he found that his armour had been stolen and he could not remember his name. He wandered in the forest until Beleare found him, nursed him back to health and, her husband being presumed killed by the creature, married Gwigalois and bore him twin sons.

25th September

For a long while Lancelot agonized over the matter of his love for the Queen. As time passed and the influence of Mordred began to sap the strength of the Round Table like a canker in a wound, so he came to believe that he must end the love of so many years for the good of the kingdom. And thereby he sent word to the Queen that he would see her in her chamber. They talked long, and wept not a little, but finally agreed that they would meet in secret no longer. Thus it might have been that the evil things which were to follow were avoided; Mordred and Agravain his brother, however, had spied upon Lancelot and at this moment they began to hammer on the door demanding to be admitted. And since there was no other way, Lancelot was forced to defend himself, slaying Agravain outside the chamber along with ten other knights, and wounding Mordred sorely. Then Lancelot fled, for he knew that all was over now for himself and the Queen.   ▷

26th September

Mordred went to the King and told his tale and Arthur, eaten by sorrow, was forced to arraign the Queen. The verdict was inevitable. Arthur himself decreed that she be sentenced to burn at the stake. But secretly he sent word to Lancelot to save the woman they both loved.   ▷ 29TH SEPTEMBER

27th September

Bors, Perceval, Galahad and Dindrane left the Ship of Solomon and rode together. Suddenly they were surrounded by a host of men who attempted to capture Dindrane. 'Give us the maiden, for she must observe the custom of this place and fill a dish brimful with her blood.' All were incensed at this, but Dindrane said, 'I will go gladly, since Our Lord bids me enter without fear.' They went in and heard how the lady of that castle was wasting away with leprosy and that only a basin of maiden's blood might cure her. Though many had suffered this bleeding, none had sufficient virtue to effect healing. Dindrane went and spoke to the lady and returned. 'Be of good heart, I am resolved in this matter.' And despite their pleading, she remained adamant.   ▷

28th September

After hearing Mass, Dindrane bade farewell to each of the Grail company. Then she let them open her arm and they watched aghast as the blood filled the bowl. With her last breath, Dindrane said to Perceval, 'Brother, do not bury me here. Take me with you to Sarras.' And as the Grail knights wept, so

Perceval's sister Dindrane, having given her life-blood to heal a leprous lady, expires, watched by her brother, Galahad and Bors and the people of the sick woman's castle.

Dindrane died. The blood was brought to the leprous lady, who washed in it and was made whole again. Then the Grail knights laid Dindrane's body in the Ship of Solomon. And never were men so heavy of heart as they. ▷ 28TH FEBRUARY

───────── 29th September ─────────

*O*n the morning of the dark day when the Queen must burn, a silent crowd gathered in the courtyard of Camelot. All there were grim, and Gawain would not attend. His brothers, Gareth and Gaheries, went with the guard on the Queen, but went unarmed in token of their faith in her. Thus was their fate sealed, for Lancelot came at the hour of execution and carried off the Queen. And in the mêlée many knights fell, including Gareth and Gaheries. ▷

───────── 30th September ─────────

*W*hen word of this was brought to Gawain, he went before Arthur, tears of sorrow and anger upon his cheeks, and demanded that he pursue Lancelot and make war upon him. Nor might Arthur gainsay him, for he was become like a candle in the wind with all that had occurred. ▷ 21ST OCTOBER

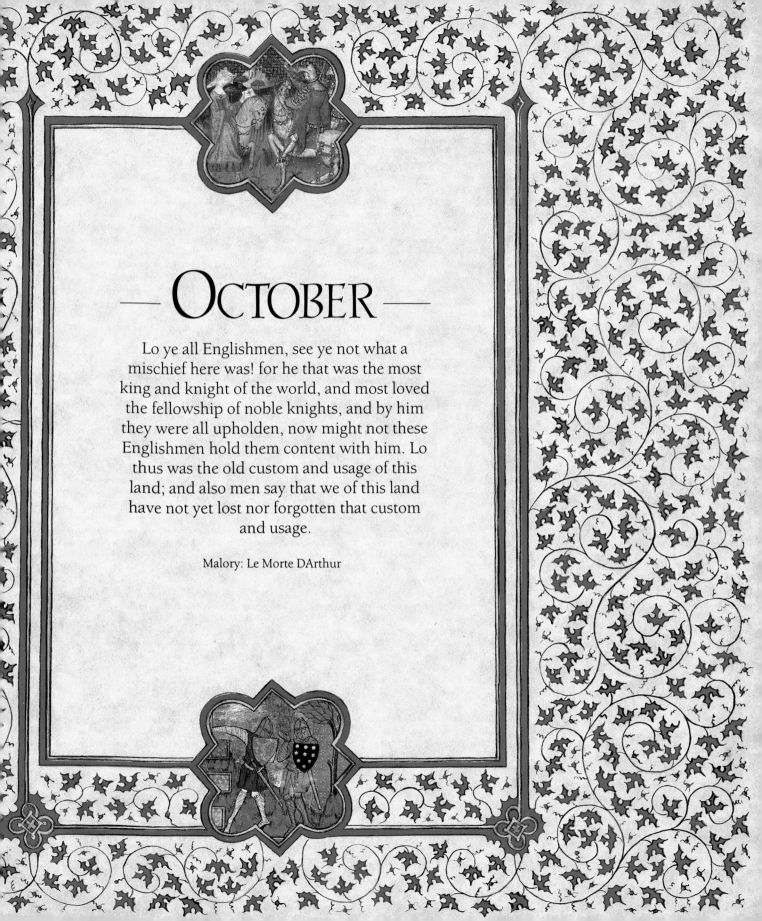

OCTOBER

Lo ye all Englishmen, see ye not what a
mischief here was! for he that was the most
king and knight of the world, and most loved
the fellowship of noble knights, and by him
they were all upholden, now might not these
Englishmen hold them content with him. Lo
thus was the old custom and usage of this
land; and also men say that we of this land
have not yet lost nor forgotten that custom
and usage.

Malory: Le Morte DArthur

1st October

Gawain and Ector came to the Perilous Cemetery. They saw where a number of tombs burned with a seemingly eternal flame. On a stone by the door was written that only the bravest of the brave could douse the flames. They entered, but were turned back by a dozen swords which, wielded by no visible opponent, flew up from the tombs and attacked them. Neither dared venture within again and it was left to Lancelot to bring an end to the mystery on another day.

Gawain and Ector try the adventure of the Perilous Cemetery, only to be rebuffed by its strange and unearthly defenders. Here, flames and swords rise from the tombs, and the knights retreat, Ector with five swords stuck in his shield.

2nd October

Perceval had met with no living being for many months and so he was glad to come upon a hermit's cell. Perceval asked him the meaning of his dreams. The hermit had got good account of Perceval's life and spoke to this effect: 'You seem to have ever been in service to the creaturely world which has appeared to you in the semblance of woman. Your care has been for the world's pain, which is denoted by the great pit full of crying. The good God has willed that you learn skill in arms from a witch and still come to no scathe. The world has appeared to you in these two guises: the witch on the dragon and the maiden on the lion. They are the old law of creaturely kind and the new law which Christ our Lord has established. Be easy in your mind, for soon you will encounter the knights Bors and Galahad and then you shall find what you have been seeking.'

3rd October

Eleyne led Fair Unknown to the castle of Sinadoun, where her lady lay imprisoned. Although she had mocked his inexperience, she now knew him to be a proven man of strength, for he had defended her in countless adventures. Fair Unknown fought with the two clerks who held the lady prisoner by their

enchantment. He wounded one and killed the other and then burst into the room where the lady was. He was astounded to see a griffin with a woman's face. It came across the floor towards him, wrapped itself about him and kissed him. Immediately, a naked woman stood before him and he rushed from the chamber, calling upon Eleyne to bring clothes. The griffin was none other than the Lady of Sinadoun herself. 'For I was enchanted by these two clerks as you saw, and I was destined to remain in that loathly shape until I could kiss Gawain or one of his close kin.' ▷

─────────── 4th October ───────────

*T*hey returned to Glastonbury and there Morgain le Fay uncovered the mystery. 'I can tell who you are. Fair Unknown no more, you are Guingelain, the son of Gawain and a faery woman,' said Morgain. 'Your mother wished you to remain with her in faery, but your father's blood gave you a love of chivalry and high deeds.' Then Gawain kissed his son and welcomed the Lady of Sinadoun, who in a joyful ceremony became his daughter-in-law before the court returned to Camelot.

─────────── 5th October ───────────

*O*ne morning Gawain met a messenger hastening to Camelot. He came, the man revealed, from King Flois, who needed help from Arthur against a giant who had appeared and was terrorizing his lands. 'Look no further,' Gawain said, 'I shall accompany you.' But on the way he was welcomed at the castle of the maiden Amurfina, who had for long loved him secretly and now requested his championship against her sister. When he deliberated she gave him a potion which caused him to lose his memory for three weeks. Then, one morning, happening to catch sight of his shield, he all of a sudden remembered who he was and the nature of his task, and left that place without further delay. At length he arrived at the castle of King Flois and using all his skill and cunning and almost supernatural power he was able to slay the giant after a furious battle. He then set off to return to Camelot. ▷

─────────── 6th October ───────────

*O*n the way he encountered Sir Kay, who had been persuaded to take up the quarrel of Amurfina's sister, but had turned back at a perilous bridge. Not knowing the identity of the maiden with Kay, Gawain undertook the battle for her, but on realizing that it was Amurfina he fought against, he changed sides: in

truth he loved the maiden more than her sister. Gawain then persuaded the two women to accompany him to Camelot and to let Arthur decide the quarrel. This was accomplished amicably and Gawain returned with Amurfina to her castle, where he remained for some time, taking pleasure in her company.

7th October

When Tristan had been at the court of Hoel of Brittany for a year, had married his daughter and helped him against his enemies, there came a messenger whom he recognized. It was Brangane, Isolt of Ireland's handmaid. All the colour left Tristan's face when he saw her, and he opened the letter with a trembling hand. Within he read the message: 'Tristan, you have given me great pain. How long will you remain away from me? Come home, my love, come home.' Kaherdin, who was near at hand, saw the look upon his friend's face, and

Brangane brings a message to Tristan from Isolt asking him to come home. Kaherdin, riding beside him, knows that he will go, deserting his wife Isolt of Brittany.

knew at once that he was going to depart. He said: 'Take care, Tristan, for you surely have many enemies in Cornwall.' But Tristan only looked at him with blind eyes and heard him not. Next day he departed for Britain with Brangane.

▷ 14TH DECEMBER

─────── 8th October ───────

On the death of King Ambrosius, there appeared over Britain a great comet in the shape of a dragon. From its mouth issued two rays of light. Uther, the King's brother, was out hunting and he summoned Merlin to tell him what this portent signified. 'Noble lord, your brother is dead. Hasten now to claim the crown of Britain. The starry dragon signifies yourself. The first beam denotes your son, who will be the greatest king this land has ever known; the second ray denotes your daughter, whose sons and grandsons will succeed to the kingship of Britain.' Thus it was that the Dragon became the emblem of Arthur's reign, its image rearing over the field of battle. Yet this glorious vision also prefigured the downfall of Arthur and the barrenness of his own line.

▷ 21ST MARCH

─────── 9th October ───────

Dwellers from the Otherworld often found their way to Arthur's court, bringing either treasure or trial according to their kind. One of the strangest was the lady Leithe, of whom it was by chance revealed that she had a tuft of grey hair sprouting behind her right knee. Now the truth of the matter was that this was a sign of her faery origins, and of her power to change her shape into that of a grey cat, but such things are not meant to be mooted openly, and the lady was so angered that she caused similar tufts to appear behind the knees of every other woman in the court – though not with the same property as her own. Then, for she was no mean sorceress, she visited upon the whole court a dream of such fearsome reality that many almost died of it. In this dream they were all transported to the Otherworld, where they were set upon and killed by a horde of monstrous cats. It may be that none would have woken from the dream had not Gawain, wise in the matters of the Otherworld, begun to slay the cats in vast numbers. At length the lady Leithe held up her hand, and at once all the dead knights returned to life and found themselves in the arms of beautiful maidens who loved them sweetly until morning. Then they awoke to find that Leithe herself had vanished and that the tufts of grey hair were also gone from their own women. But they never forgot the dream and were ever after cautious as to making even the most innocuous and casual remarks about the appearance of the people of the Otherworld.

──── ◇ ────

'YOUR DAUGHTER': MORGAUSE, DAUGHTER OF GORLOIS AND IGRAIN AND STEPDAUGHTER OF UTHER

──── ◇ ────

10th October

Gawain's fame as a lover was legendary. Once, he entered the bedchamber of the Lady of Norgalles, having first successfully negotiated an ante-room in which four armed knights kept guard. Extinguishing the lighted taper which burned in the outer room, Gawain reached his goal. Later he was forced to fight with twenty knights as a result of his night's pleasure. But he beat them all, and the lady was by no means displeased.

11th October

Lancelot came to the Castle of Griffins, where there was a custom that whoever came there must try to pull forth a spear embedded in the wall. He did so, but refused to marry the daughter of the castle and was thrown into prison. From there he obtained release with the help of a magical dog, given to him by a maiden. Beyond the castle he came to a barge which carried him to an island. There he saw two great tombs prepared on which were the names of Arthur and Guinevere. He wept, and heard a voice proclaim that this was Avalon, where all were re-united in love and life. Thus cheered, Lancelot went on his way.

12th October

It was the custom of Arthur to bestow upon his followers gifts according to their prowess and their meed. It so happened that the father of Sir Launfal had been one of those men who opposed the kingship of Arthur and had lived in uneasy peace. Poor Launfal therefore came with little recommendation and, despite his attempts to win Arthur's notice, it seemed that he of all men had least reward. Yet he was a handsome youth and knew himself to be brave and courteous, and so he decided to go adventuring alone and win fame as well he might. ▷

Gawain is entertained by the Lady of Norgalles. He enters the chamber in which her guards sleep and extinguishes a candle burning there. In the second picture he is kissing the lady, who is naked in her bed.

MEED: MERIT

13th October

Launfal travelled until he crossed a stream and saw a company of ravishingly beautiful maidens dancing on the shore. They were dressed in green, which should have told him that they were faery women. He joined their dance and they led him to a pavilion of richest gold. Seated within was the Queen of Faery herself, her skin as white as hawthorn-blossom and her lips as red as rowanberries. She smiled on Launfal and gave him a gift: a purse which would never be empty. He thanked her gratefully and begged to be allowed to serve her. 'So shall you, Launfal, for I take you as my love. But I set a condition upon you – that you never speak of me to another or you will lose me forever.' Launfal promised faithfully to abide by this, and remained with her for a year, enjoying the delights of the Otherworld and the sweetness of the Faery Queen's love. ▷

14th October

It happened that Guinevere and her companions came to that very spot a year later in order to pick berries. The day was fine and they were merry. Launfal heard their voices and strayed into their company to watch the ladies and their pages dancing. Guinevere noticed him. 'Why, Sir Launfal, it is long since we saw you. Will you not dance with me here?' To Launfal's eyes the ladies looked like serving-maids and the Queen like a cook; their revels seemed uncouth compared to his year's revelling in Faery. 'Madam, excuse me, but I would rather not.' The Queen, affronted by this response and unable to believe the evidence of her ears, demanded to know the reason. 'Madam, my lady's companions exceed you so far in beauty that I would not waste my time.' Guinevere was outraged and ordered Launfal seized and brought to trial. ▷

15th October

Launfal came before Arthur and his peers, and there Guinevere blushed to repeat the calumny which Launfal had uttered against her. While Arthur was debating what judgement to bring, the Faery Queen herself arrived. She was dressed in white and gold, and brought the breath of spring in her train. It was plain to the eyes of the most dim-sighted that she surpassed the Queen, so beautiful was she. 'My judgement is this, Sir Launfal,' said Arthur. 'You spoke the truth about this lady's beauty, but so basely did you utter it that this court cannot abide your presence longer. Go wherever you like, so long as you leave my kingdom.' And the Faery Queen said to Arthur: 'Lord King, because of a promise which Launfal made and broke, I also judge that he will never more be seen in mortal lands, but he will remain with me in bliss.' And so it was.

16th October

Perceval rode on his adventures and came to a castle where much lamenting was heard. 'What is this place?' he enquired. 'This is the castle of the King of the Court of Suffering,' wept a woman, 'see!' And she pointed to where a doleful king came leading three white horses. Over each crupper was a dead man. Perceval watched amazed as the dead men were swung down, bathed in cauldrons of water and then anointed with balm. Each sprang up alive, but no one rejoiced at this miracle. 'Each day my three sons undergo this torment,' said the King. 'An avanc, a dreadful beast, kills them and each night they remain dead until I bring their bodies back to be restored.' Perceval immediately wanted to overcome the avanc and rode off in search of it. A beautiful woman appeared to him in a dream, the same he had seen once before in his vision of the blood in the snow. 'Promise to love me and I will give you a ring of invisibility to overcome the beast.' When he awoke, the ring was on his hand. He waited by the beast's cave until just before the King's three sons rode by, and then darted out and plunged his sword into its throat. The loathsome monster lay dead and the household of the King of the Court of Suffering was released from its torment.

17th October

Owain had been gone so long that Arthur and his men went off in search of him, following Colgrevance. They found the King of the Animals and the fountain, where Kay insisted on being the one to make the challenge. He cast the water upon the stone and caused such a thunderstorm that several of Arthur's attendants were slain by hailstones. The black knight of the fountain came riding up and soon overthrew Kay. Gawain then fought the black knight. They battled for a long time, equally matched, until the black knight struck Gawain's helmet from his head. Immediately Owain recognized his friend. Arthur commanded that Owain return with them, and he gladly followed them to Camelot. ▷

18th October

Owain went away without thought of his lady. He was eating his dinner when Luned rode into the hall: 'Faithless and deceitful; be thou disgraced and without honour!' As she cursed him, Luned stripped the ring from his finger. Immediately Owain gave a cry, sprang up and rushed from the hall. Madness came upon him and, in his unreason, he wandered for a long time in the wilderness, unknowing and uncaring of chivalry. His hair and beard grew shaggy like a beast's and he was reduced to scraping in the ground for roots and to eating raw meat. And so he continued for many months. ▷ 19TH AUGUST

19th October

While Luned took service with the Countess Laudine, Owain lurked in the woods nearby. Such was his sad condition that he could not return to Camelot without great restoration. So it was that Luned pretended to discover Owain lying in the Countess' garden. She exclaimed at the condition of the poor knight's wounds and his utter dereliction. The Countess was a woman of soft heart and she enjoyed tending to the mazed knight, who was obviously of such good lineage. She was possessed of a healing balm, which Morgain le Fay had given her, for the Countess frequently consulted the enchantress on many matters. Luned was so concerned for Owain's recovery that she used nearly the whole phial upon him, which caused Laudine to dismiss her. But thanks to her ministrations Owain made a complete recovery and now, freshly attired and barbered, he went on his way. ▷

MAZED: BEWILDERED

20th October

Owain and Luned made their way to the realm of the Fountain with sadness. Owain was still married to its Lady, though he had grown to return Luned's affection. As they approached, it appeared that all was not well there. The castle was uninhabited and the Fountain clogged and muddy. They came upon the King of the Animals, who told them that the Lady of the Fountain had died of grief from the loss of her champion. 'Then let the challenge of the Fountain be no more,' said Owain. 'And let us return to Camelot in peace. And you,' he said to the black man with one eye, 'shall be undisputed lord of this kingdom, for I have dwelt as a beast and been companioned by a beast. Let this kingdom belong to them, and trouble the world of men no more.'

21st October

For three months the forces of Arthur and Gawain besieged Joyous Gard. Then came representatives from the Pope demanding that the King put an end to these hostilities and take back the Queen. At first Gawain ranted against any such agreement, but then it was learned that Guinevere had never been inside Joyous Gard at all: Lancelot had entrusted her to the care of the Holy Sisters at Amesbury directly after he had rescued her. He swore to uphold her faithfulness to Arthur by the strength of his body, which all knew could not be overcome. So Arthur bowed willingly to the request of the Pope and forced Gawain to agree. With due ceremony Guinevere was restored fully to her royal place, but Lancelot was banished, being given six days to depart forever from the kingdom and all lands that belonged to Arthur. ▷

22nd October

*E*ven this was not enough to satisfy Gawain's lust for vengeance. Within a week of Lancelot's departure for Benoic, he was demanding that Arthur gather an army to pursue the once greatest knight of the Round Table across the Channel. Arthur conceded, because he knew that there was blood-hunger in the air, and this was as good a way as any to appease it. So he established Mordred as regent in his absence, and crossed the sea in a vast armada of ships. ▷

23rd October

*F*or long months the siege dragged on. Every day Gawain stood before the walls and taunted Lancelot until the great knight came forth to do battle with him. And every day Gawain was laid low, though never would Lancelot hurt him in any way beyond knocking him from his horse. But at last the two friends fought in earnest, and Lancelot was forced to use the power of his sword-arm against Gawain. The resulting head-wound laid him low for a week, when word came from Britain of a disturbing nature. ▷

24th October

*M*ordred, Arthur's bastard son, whom he had once tried to have killed, but to whom he had given cautious but increasing trust, had declared Arthur and Gawain dead, and made himself king. Guinevere had shut herself up in the Tower of London, to which Mordred now laid siege. ▷

25th October

*A*rthur gathered his forces to return at once to Britain. They landed at Dover, and there, as a result of his wounds, Gawain died. He wrote a last letter to Lancelot, begging forgiveness, and asking that he pray for his spirit. ▷

26th October

*T*he army marched north and west towards where they knew Mordred to be massing his forces. With them went the body of Gawain. As they passed the castle of a lord named Marin, his lady, who had long loved Gawain in secret, learned that her love's body was in the van and came, crying and weeping, to walk behind the bier. Her lord, mad with jealousy, ran after her and slew her before the eyes of the army. Arthur ordered him hanged by the wayside, as a warning that such jealous acts were still forbidden in his lands. ▷

Before the battle of Camlan Guinevere retires to a nunnery. She is shown here being welcomed by the Mother Abbess and her sisters.

27th October

*L*earning of the King's approach, Mordred fled northwards. Queen Guinevere, no longer besieged, came out of London to meet her lord. There, in the winter dawn, Arthur and his Queen were finally reconciled. And if tears were shed upon either side, the books make no mention of it. Then as Arthur prepared for battle, the Queen, filled with dread and sorrow, took leave of her lord and returned to Amesbury. ▷

28th October

*T*he forces of Arthur and Mordred encamped near to the place called Camlan, which in the British tongue means 'Crooked Bank'. That night Arthur dreamed that he sat on the top of Fortune's Wheel and that the wheel turned, throwing him down. Then came the spirit of Gawain, surrounded by the fair ladies he had helped in his life, who warned him not to fight next day. ▷

The night before the battle of Camlan Arthur dreams of the Goddess Fortune, seeing himself on the wheel, which turns, unsettling him as it does all men.

*T*he morning of the battle dawned dark and stormy. On one side King Arthur's host was drawn up in battle array, its numbers small. Ranged against them were Mordred's forces, mostly Saxon tribesmen, their numbers swelled by the addition of traitorous knights for whom the Round Table was but the childish dream of an old and powerless king.

Before the battle Mordred exhorted his men: 'Slay any who confront you. Take no hostages. Do not let your hearts be swayed by ancient ties of blood.'

The King also addressed his forces: 'I am glad this day has come, for now we can right an old wrong, and rid this land finally of treachery and evil persuasion. My knights and kinsmen, though we die today, let none say that the Round Table died with us.'

Before the standards were raised, the seneschals of either side sought to make peace. While terms were discussed, men on either side laid down their arms to find water. One knight, dismounting, was bitten by an adder that darted forth from the bushes. But when he drew his sword to slay it, both sides saw the flash of his blade and thought they saw treachery. And so, unprepared and

The Battle of Camlan, portrayed here in all its blood and horror. Men lie dead in heaps around Arthur, who lies wounded in the bottom right-hand corner of the picture.

headlong, the two armies cast themselves into the fray, the White Horse banner of the Saxons and the White Dragon of Mordred against the Draco of King Arthur Pendragon.

All that day the battle raged, with little pause, and always, amid a steadily diminishing island of men, Arthur fought on, wielding Excalibur until its silver blade was dark with blood. And ever he looked for Mordred among the faces of his foes.

At last he saw his son, leaning on his sword among a heap of dead men. 'This day shall have its ending,' swore Arthur, and bade his armour-bearer, Sir Lucan, bring his spear. 'My lord, spare your hand and remember the warning of Sir Gawain,' said Lucan. 'Come life, come death, that traitor shall not escape the field,' cried Arthur.

Mordred raised his head, shaking the blood from his eyes, to see his father with the spear. 'You have done well,' he said, 'better than I believed. Now do you go hunting the boar, father?' and he laughed.

'Sword against men, spear against swine,' replied Arthur, his face set for slaughter. And seeing his chance, for Mordred raised his shield too high, he thrust under the skirts of his son's armour into his belly.

Feeling the dark pull of the death-stroke in his groin, Mordred cast himself upon the spear, the better to reach his father. Like any wild boar at bay, he thrust himself the length of the spear and raised his sword, bringing it down upon his father's helm. Sword and helmet burst in twain and father and son fell amid the great heap of dead.

From that ghastly mêlée, Lucan and Bedivere pulled forth the body of the King, to find him yet breathing, though terribly wounded. They carried him away from the blood-soaked field and laid him on cool grass, with a shield for pillow. And they sat with him, sore afraid that he must die.　　▷

─────── 30th October ───────

*T*hen Arthur groaned and opened his eyes, and seeing where Sir Bedivere stood close by, Sir Lucan having departed in search of help, he said: 'Take thou Excalibur and cast it into the lake that is nearby.' And Bedivere went to where the still, flat water lay like bloody steel under the setting sun, but he could not do as he had been asked. Twice he returned and twice more Arthur sent him forth, until at last he did as he was bid and flung the great sword out into the water. And lo! a hand and an arm, clothed in samite, rose from the water, and caught the sword, and brandished it thrice, and then withdrew it beneath the surface. When he heard this Arthur gave a long sigh, and stretched himself out on the earth as if he would die.　　▷

The wounded Arthur awaits the return of Bedivere, who, after throwing the sword Excalibur into the lake, watches as a mysterious arm and hand rise from the water and grasp it. (30th October)

31st October

*T*hen came Sir Lucan, and the two carried the King to the shore. In so doing, Sir Lucan's own wounds burst open and he fell dying. Bedivere paused to succour him, and when next he looked where the King was laid he saw Arthur staring out to sea. There came a ship with a black sail and on the deck were three women with golden crowns: Morgain le Fay, the Queen of the Outer Isles, and the Queen of Norgalles. And he drew his sword, for all were enemies of the King. But Arthur whispered, 'Fear not, Bedivere, these women are come to bear me to Avalon, where I shall be healed of my wounds. Return to Camelot, salvage what you can, keep alive the old ways.' The King's breath came ragged: 'Remember me to Sir Lancelot, and to the Queen. They were ever faithful to my name.' Then he spoke no more, but submitted himself to be lifted aboard the ship. Bedivere watched as the King was carried from his sight, and he wept to see the departing of the best that ever sat upon a throne in the Island of the Mighty.

▷ 2ND NOVEMBER

– November –

Whatever the weather might be, the meadow
and the wood were always like summer . . . If
anyone who was suffering grief traversed
these two places, he was filled with such joy
that he forgot his sadness. For that reason
they called the wood Beforet, the Beautiful
Wood, so manifold were its beauties . . .
Lions, bears, red deer, boars and whatever
one could wish to hunt were there in
numbers more than enough for good sport.

Lanzelet

The Conception of Merlin. In Hell a devilish council is plotting the birth of Antichrist. One of their number, dispatched to the world above, lies with a virgin to beget Merlin.

1st November

*I*t was as Vortigern's messengers scoured the kingdom that two came to Caer Merddin and overheard some boys taunting one of their number for his birth: 'We are of noble blood: as for you, no one even knows who your father was!' The messengers seized the boy and brought him with his mother before Vortigern. He questioned the mother closely. She was a princess of Demetia, a professed nun. She said: 'A handsome young man would often come to me in my cell and embrace me. I never knew where he came from, nor who he was. Sometimes he would be invisible and just speak with me; at other times, we lay together, and it was so that I conceived this boy, whom I call Merlin Emrys.' 'It is clear,' said the chief Druid, 'that this woman had has relations with a spirit of the air. These daemons frequently assume mortal guise and lie with women.' So it was that Vortigern discovered the sacrifice he sought: a boy without a father.

▷ 29TH AUGUST

2nd November

*W*hen the news reached Lancelot in France of the great battle between Arthur and Mordred, he hastened to Britain as fast as ship could carry him. But the battle was long over by the time he came there, and word of Arthur's departing was everywhere on the wind. And so he wandered for a time, too heartsick to know where he should go, until he found himself at a hermitage, where he found Sir Bors and the old Archbishop of Canterbury. And there he stayed, putting off his armour and laying aside his sword. Thus he became a hermit, dwelling in the wilderness, and there his brother Sir Ector came and stayed with him.

▷ 27TH DECEMBER

3rd November

*T*here was a young knight named Bleoberis who loved a lady of passing great beauty. When he went to her and declared his feelings she smiled upon him but said: 'I will only be yours if you achieve a quest that I will set upon you. You must go to the court of King Arthur and bring me the hawk that sits upon a golden perch in the great hall of the Round Table.' And Sir Bleoberis promised her and set out.

He had not gone very far before he came upon a lady mounted on a horse at a crossroads. She addressed him thus: 'Sir knight: I know upon what quest you are engaged, and I tell you that you can only succeed with my help.' 'What must I do?' asked Bleoberis. 'First you must take my horse, which will lead you where you desire to go. Then you must find and take a golden glove that hangs on a

pillar in the castle of the giant Bran. If you succeed in this you shall be able to carry off the hawk – assuming, that is, that you can also defeat the twelve knights of the Round Table who guard it.' So Bleoberis took the lady's mount and let it take him where it would. ▷

4th November

*N*ext *day he reached a castle. It was surrounded by a turbulent lake, and the only way over was across a narrow bridge which dipped beneath the surface and trembled continually with the motion of the water. Then Bleoberis saw a tall figure in armour appear at the far end and stand waiting. He knew what he must do. Drawing his sword, he rushed across the bridge, not thinking about its narrowness, and engaged furiously in combat with the guardian knight. After a long fight he slew him and entered the castle. Within, it was dim and cool and he found a table laid with food. Hungry and tired, he fell upon it without thought, but before he had taken more than a bite a huge figure crashed into the hall. Almost a giant, waving a great club, he was of fearsome aspect. 'Have you no manners, boy?' he bellowed. 'Dare you to come in here and take what you wish?' 'I have come for more than food,' answered Bleoberis boldly. 'I have come for the gauntlet which hangs from the pillar of gold.' 'Then prepare to defend yourself, for I am its guardian and no man may overcome me.' Bleoberis and the giant fought for several hours, until at last the knight slipped beneath the guard of his opponent and struck off his hand, club and all. Bellowing with pain the creature begged for mercy, and took Bleoberis to where the gauntlet hung. The knight took it down and left the castle as swiftly as possible, turning towards Camelot.* ▷

5th November

*B*leoberis *reached the fabled city of Arthur next day, and there was met by twelve knights, who challenged his right to enter. Bleoberis raised his hand, on which was the golden glove, and said: 'By the right of this glove I seek the hawk which sits in the hall of the Round Table.' 'Why so?' demanded the leader of the knights. 'To prove that my lady is fairer than any in this court.' 'Then defend yourself at once.' So Bleoberis fought with the twelve knights one by one and each one he unhorsed, until finally Sir Kay came forward to stop the fight, and led him inside. There he was allowed to take the hawk, which was the prize of many tournaments, and Arthur asked him to join the Round Table.*

Then Bleoberis set off for home, meeting, on the way, the mysterious lady who had helped him. 'Sir knight,' she said, 'I am glad to see that you have been successful. Go with my blessing to your true love. But remember, that if you come

this way again I shall be here, and I too am a Queen of Love,' and she faded from his sight without more words. And it is said that Bleoberis did indeed return there from time to time, for many a long year, until he was an old man and his wife dead, and that afterwards the lady came and took him to Faery, where he became ever young.

6th November
---

*I*t was a chill morning when Arthur and his court rose early to hunt for the White Hart in the Forest of Dean. He had promised Guinevere that they should ride out together, but so deeply was the Queen sleeping that the court rode out without her. When Guinevere eventually awoke and went to the stables, only two horses were left. So, accompanied only by her maid, Guinevere rode after the hunt. They rode for some time without crossing the track of any hunter. Instead they found only a tall knight, who stood menacing and unmoving in the trees. 'Go and ask who he is,' demanded Guinevere of her maid. 'You are too common to speak with me,' replied the knight and lashed the maid viciously across the face with his whip. 'Who insults her, insults me,' cried the Queen, as the knight rode away. Sir Gereint rode up and heard what had befallen. He promised to avenge Guinevere and bade her return to the safety of the court. Then, without stopping to equip himself with either arms or armour, Gereint rode off in pursuit of the insolent knight.   ▷

7th November
---

*C*lose on the track of the knight, Gereint rode until he came to a town where a great tournament was preparing, and there he saw a great knight clad in dark mail, whom all avoided. He asked of an old man, 'Who is that knight?' The man replied, 'He is Yder, the man who put me from my earldom, for I was once Earl Ynwyl. Each year he holds a tournament; for two years running he has won the sparrowhawk. If Yder wins it this year he shall become the Knight of the Sparrowhawk and hold all in his power.' 'May I contest his right and so avenge you?' asked Gereint. 'I will arm you,' said Ynwyl. 'But you must have a lady, or you may not joust.' Gereint agreed to take Ynwyl's daughter, Enid, who although dressed in rags was passing fair, as his lady, little realizing what this might betoken. He acquitted himself nobly, unhorsing Yder and himself winning the prize of the sparrowhawk. Yder knelt for mercy, which Gereint granted, sending him back to Guinevere to make satisfaction for the insult which he had put upon the Queen. So it was that Ynwyl was restored to his earldom, and he bestowed on Gereint his only child, Enid.   ▷ 12TH DECEMBER

---------- 8th November ----------

While his knights were upon the Grail Quest, Arthur bestirred himself and came at length to the Castle of the Fisher King. There he sat at the table and was served of the dish which provides the food one most desires, and he was somewhat heartened.

▷ 11TH NOVEMBER

---------- 9th November ----------

There was once a king named Ypomenes who had a son and a daughter. The former was a good and honest youth, but the latter had become enmeshed in the dark side of magic. Thus when she conceived an illicit love for her own brother she used every spell at her command to win him. When her every wile failed to win a response, she fled to the forest with a mind to kill herself. There, a creature of the nether regions appeared to her in the form of a beautiful man who promised to win her brother's favour for her in return for a night with him. The girl assented but her time with her demon lover turned her against her brother and filled her instead with hatred. Then the demon prompted her to cry 'rape' against her brother, in revenge for his refusal. This the girl did, and when her innocent sibling was found guilty she demanded that he should be torn to pieces by ravening hounds. Before his horrible death he predicted that his sister would give birth to a monster, and this would also vindicate him. ▷

---------- 10th November ----------

When her term came the girl's attendants all but died of the horror that emerged from her womb: a beast with the head of a serpent, the body of a lion, and the feet of a hart and the tail of a leopard, that had within it the sound as of thirty couple of hounds barking in its belly. It fled at once into the wood, and the King put his daughter to the question until she confessed all that had occurred. She was forthwith condemned to death by strangulation.

Thus began the story of the creature known as 'The Questing Beast', or 'Glatisant', which was pursued for many years. ▷ 3RD JUNE

---------- 11th November ----------

On the third day of Arthur's sojourn at the Castle of the Fisher King, he experienced mysterious visions of which he could not speak. But it is said that Arthur saw and underwent the five changes of the Grail and witnessed the transubstantiations of the Grail. And from that moment his hair, which had been black as a raven's wing, turned overnight to pure white.

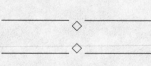

GLATISANT: FROM THE OLD FRENCH glatier, TO HOWL

TRANSUBSTANTIATIONS: THE CHANGES FROM MUNDANE TO SPIRITUAL FORM

12th November

One morning as a chill rain swept the countryside around Camelot, there came a barge down-river, draped in black. In it was laid the body of a fair young maiden, and in her hands a letter was clasped. Word spead quickly of this strange sight and Arthur himself, together with the Queen, Sir Lancelot, Sir Gawain and the rest, came down to the riverside to look. Then Arthur took up the letter and read: 'Most Noble Knight, Sir Lancelot. Now has death made an end of the debate between us. For I swear that I never loved another so well as I loved you, and that I die a clean maiden. And my last wish is that you pray for me, as you would for one that you had truly loved.'

Then Sir Lancelot wept for shame that he had caused, though all unknowing, the maiden's death, for he recognized her as Elaine of Astolat, whose favour he had carried in the tournament, and whose gentle love he had spurned. And he saw to it that she was interred with all ceremony, in a rich tomb, and prayed for her as she had wished.

A CLEAN MAIDEN: VIRGIN

Arthur and the court discover the body of Elaine, the Maid of Astolat, dead for love of Lancelot, which has floated down-river to Camelot in a barge.

13th November

*I*n a little hollow between the hills and beside the water which islanded the great Tor at Ynys Witrin, Joseph of Arimathea and his followers laboured long to build a fitting chapel to house the Holy Grail. They built a church of wattles, and painted it white so that it shone like a star against the green of the hillsides. And there the Grail rested, for a long time, until a new Guardian came to carry it to a more splendid place.

14th November

*O*ne day, in the depths of winter, there arrived at court a girl named Flordibel and her father. He gave it as his wish that his child be allowed to stay, on the condition that any man who desired her stood to lose his head. Arthur agreed, with some reluctance. When she had been there but a few months, Flordibel met Guinevere's young cousin Tandareis, and fell in love with him. Regretting the earlier condition, she agreed to flee with her lover to his father's castle.

Learning of their escape, Arthur and his men besieged the castle, demanding the return of Flordibel. Tandareis emerged to fight several of the best Round Table knights and captured them all. But he refused to fight Sir Gawain. Flordibel then gave herself up and pleaded for her lover's life. Arthur judged them innocent, but sent Tandareis away to seek adventure.   ▷

15th November

*I*n the next few months a stream of prisoners returned to Camelot – all sent by Tandareis, whose prowess they extolled. Meanwhile, while Tandareis was escorting a maiden named Claudin back to her home they were set upon by a band of renegade knights led by Kandylion. Despite a heroic struggle, Tandareis was finally overcome when Kandylion seized Claudin and threatened to rape her unless the young knight gave in. Thrown into a dungeon, Tandareis was seen by Kandylion's sister Antonie, who secretly took pity on him and helped him to escape to her own castle. There he remained for a time – long enough for Antonie to fall in love with him.   ▷

16th November

*T*andareis' thoughts turned again towards Flordibel, and when he learned that Arthur was holding a winter court nearby, where there was to be a great tournament, he requested of Antonie that he be allowed to attend. She agreed, extracting a promise from him to return to her.

In the tournament, Tandareis, in plain armour, fought well, though no one recognized him. He returned three days in succession and each time carried off the prize, escaping before he could be properly identified. But Flordibel had noticed him, and went to Arthur with the belief that the stranger knight was indeed Tandareis and that he must be held against his will. Kandylion also happened to be at court, and, guessing the identity of the knight and acknowledging his bravery, sent word to his sister to release her captive. Once assurances were given upon all sides that both Tandareis and Antonie would not be harmed, the knight returned to Camelot. There he was awarded the prize for the tournament, and Flordibel's father, relenting of his former strictures, gave his consent to their marriage. At the same time Antonie, accepting the loss of Tandareis, married Gawain's brother Gaheries, amid much rejoicing.

17th November

One afternoon Arthur announced: 'I have such tiredness upon me. Pray tell merry tales to each other while I sleep.' And he retired to a day-bed in a curtained alcove. Sir Colgrevance had but recently returned from an adventure and they begged him to tell it. Reluctantly he began: 'I travelled in wild places until I came to the edge of Faery itself. There I was pleasantly housed and attended by damsels whose beauty surpassed that of our Queen, saving her presence.' And here he bowed to Guinevere, who smiled graciously. 'I told my host that I was seeking adventure and he certainly sent me in the right direction. I came to a valley wherein was an ancient mound. Seated there was a gigantic black man with one foot and but one eye in his head. About him grazed thousands of animals, for he was the guardian of the wood. When I asked him about his power over the animals, he struck a nearby stag with his iron club so that the beast brayed loudly and called the animals to him, and they all bowed their heads to him. He then bade me go to a neighbouring valley. There I found a mighty pine-tree and under it a fountain and a green marble stone. On the stone was a silver bowl. He bade me throw a bowlful of water on this green stone, which I did, though I never would have done so had I known what dishonour would befall me afterwards. Then was there thunder, lightning and such a rain that it stripped the leaves from the tree. At once it was covered with singing birds and there came riding down the valley a great knight, he and his horse and armour all caparisoned in black. We fought for a short while but I was overcome and so returned here. Truly, if any knight lacked adventure, he would find it there.' They all commiserated with Colgrevance's bad fortune and exclaimed at his humility in telling a tale against himself. But Owain, who had listened hard to this tale, resolved to try these wonders himself. ▷ 13TH SEPTEMBER

◇

Colgrevance tells the tale of his encounter with the Wild Herdsman at the Fountain of Barenton. Arthur and the court listen enthralled.

◇

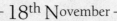

--- 18th November ---

There were once two friends named Claris and Laris who set out on a journey from a distant part of the land to find the court of the famed King Arthur, of whom they had heard so many rumours and tales. As they rode, Claris confessed his love for Lidoine, the daughter of an aged king in a neighbouring realm. Laris in turn promised to help his friend and told him of the love he bore for Marine, the daughter of King Uriens of Gore. Claris also promised to help his friend, but it was to be long before either could fulfil his promise, for soon afterwards Laris, sleeping, was carried off by Madoine, a sorceress of Morgain le Fay. ▷

--- 19th November ---

Claris, distressed, set out in search of his friend and after many adventures arrived in the Valley of No Return, where lay Morgain's palace of pleasures. Here Claris too was captured, this time by Morgain herself, who desired the young knight greatly. The two friends might have remained in prison for many more years had not Laris prevailed upon Madoine, who really loved him, to set them both free. ▷ 24TH NOVEMBER

--- 20th November ---

Morgain le Fay was ever determined to bring harm to her brother King Arthur. When she learned of the power that was in the sword Excalibur and the scabbard that were given by the Lady of the Lake, she devised a way to steal them both and to send them to her lover, Accolon of Gaul. Therefore, when Arthur and many other knights of the Round Table were hunting one day, it happened that the King, together with Accolon and King Uriens of Gore, became separated from the rest as night fell. They came to a river where a great barge was moored. They went aboard and there found damsels who served them with wine and rich food. And since there seemed no harm in them the King and his knights accepted their hospitality and retired to rest upon comfortable beds. But in the morning Uriens found himself in bed with his wife Morgain le Fay, while Arthur found himself in a dungeon with other knight prisoners, and Sir Accolon found himself by a deep well, with a messenger in attendance who bore in his arms a bundle wrapped in silk. Within it was Excalibur, its blade catching the morning light in points of fire. 'Here,' said the messenger, 'Your lady, Morgain le Fay, sends this to you and bids you remember your love for each other and that you will do as you had planned with this sword.' For Morgain and Accolon had long plotted to murder King Arthur and thus by her magic had Morgain contrived this whole adventure. ▷

21st November

Meanwhile, in the dungeon, a damsel came to Arthur and promised to do all she might to set him free. Though he suspected nothing, she was in truth one of the damsels of Morgain le Fay. And later she came again to Arthur and said that there was a way to escape, and she would help all the other prisoners in that castle also. 'If you agree to fight a certain knight that is waiting nearby, and if you win the fight with him, then you and all these other prisoners shall be let out.' To this Arthur agreed. With his armour back and a sword which appeared to be Excalibur, he went forth to the well, where Accolon waited in plain armour and with his visor down. Then Arthur drew his sword and Accolon his and the two came together with a great crash. They fought long and hard and whenever Accolon struck Arthur he made blood flow, but whenever Arthur struck Accolon he was not even scratched. By this sign he knew that something was wrong, but he still did not guess what until in a furious counter-stroke his own sword broke. Then he knew what had occurred, and feared for his life. But it so happened that Accolon slipped on the blood which had stained the grass, and as he fell the sword flew from his grasp towards Arthur, like a bird returning to its nest. Arthur took it and at once knew that this was his own sword. Then he furiously fell upon Sir Accolon. Snatching the scabbard from him, he threw it to one side and then struck him a great blow with Excalibur which was to be his death-blow. But Accolon did not die immediately. He lived to tell Arthur of the plot his sister Morgain had made and of the hatred she bore for her brother. ▷

22nd November

Then Arthur sent the body of her lover Accolon to Morgain with the following message. 'Here is something that belongs to you. And know that I have again my sword and the scabbard.' When she received this message Morgain was beside herself with anger, and, using all her dark powers of enchantment to effect a change in her appearance, she went at once to Camelot. There, while Arthur slept, she succeeded in stealing the scabbard again, but she might not get the sword because Arthur slept with it in his hand. ▷

23rd November

When Arthur woke and was aware of his loss he set out with a party of knights in pursuit. They perceived Morgain and she them, but she fled into a valley and there, by her arts, transformed herself and her attendants into the shape of great stones, so that all who passed by thought them to be the work of the ancients. So Arthur rode past her and did not know she was there, and when he

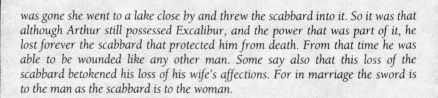

was gone she went to a lake close by and threw the scabbard into it. So it was that although Arthur still possessed Excalibur, and the power that was part of it, he lost forever the scabbard that protected him from death. From that time he was able to be wounded like any other man. Some say also that this loss of the scabbard betokened his loss of his wife's affections. For in marriage the sword is to the man as the scabbard is to the woman.

24th November

*T*he adventures of Claris and Laris were by no means over when they escaped from the castle of Morgain le Fay. They arrived at length at Arthur's court, in time to learn that King Uriens, the father of Laris' love, was besieged by an evil king. The friends begged leave of Arthur to lead the rescue party, which included both Owain and Gawain. A great number of skirmishes followed, in one of which Laris was captured. When the enemy at last admitted defeat, he was nowhere to be found, and Claris set out in search of him. ▷

25th November

*A*fter long months of searching Claris finally found Laris. He had in fact been rescued already by Madoine, who was once again reluctant to release the man she desired. In the end Claris' plea prevailed and Laris returned to seek the daughter of Uriens, who now looked with favour on the knight who had helped him to overcome his enemies. Claris, sadly enquiring after his own love, learned that her husband had died the winter before, and he returned to find her waiting for him. A double wedding was celebrated, with Claris marrying Lidoine and Laris Marine.

26th November

*M*orgause was the second daughter of Gorlois of Cornwall and Igrain. She had remained with her mother after her father's death, and thus came to meet Lot of Orkney, who was held as a hostage by Uther Pendragon. Soon Morgause fell in with the handsome youth, and in secret they became lovers. For several months they managed to meet without anyone discovering their assignations. Then Morgause discovered that she was pregnant. In fear of Uther's wrath, she retired to her rooms pleading ill-health and gave birth to a strong son in secret. She named him Gawain and gave him into the hands of a good old knight, clothing him in rich garments, with letters detailing his true lineage and a ring which either she or Lot would recognize again. ▷

27th November

*A*s fortune would have it, Gawain's foster-father was robbed by pirates and the child stolen as well, the rich clothes in which he was wrapped promising a ransom. But the pirates themselves were wrecked soon after. The child of Morgause and Lot was discovered and brought up by a merchant named Viamundus, who grew rich upon the goods he had salvaged from the pirate wreck. He soon moved to Rome, where he became known for his wisdom and honesty and was brought to the attention of the Emperor. Gawain, as the 'son' of Viamundus, joined the Imperial Guard and soon rose to a position of responsibility because of his daring and strength. At that time Viamundus fell sick and seemed like to die. Then he called to him the Emperor's advisers and told them the true identity of the young hero, showing them the letters and the ring which Morgause had entrusted to the knight. Thereupon the good merchant breathed his last. Gawain, anxious to learn more of his parents, and hearing also of the great deeds being accomplished by King Arthur, who unknown to him was his uncle, set out for the shores of Britain. ▷ 6TH JULY

28th November

*C*larine's son rode out into the world from his seclusion on the Lake island. He soon found that the best knight in the world was none other than Iweret, and so he came to that knight's domains, wondering why the Lady of the Lake had sent him out nameless. Clarine's son rode near Schatel le Mort, where he was captured by Mabuz the Cowardly. This knight was none other than the Lady of the Lake's own son. It had been prophesied that Mabuz would be a coward, so his mother had contrived a place of special safety for him in the lands of the Beautiful Wood, but Iweret had usurped this domain. This was the wrong which she had sent Clarine's son to remedy. Mabuz loved to capture brave knights and kill them. ▷

29th November

*C*larine's son languished in the dungeons of Schatel le Mort, uncaring of his courtly upbringing and sunk in total despair. The nature of that castle was to render cowardly all within it save only Mabuz, whom the walls secured from such baseness. The fellow captives of Clarine's son began to call out that Iweret had come to attack Schatel le Mort. Mabuz chose Clarine's son to ride out and defend him and bring him word of Iweret's movements. This the young man agreed to do, provided that Mabuz forbore from his custom of indiscriminate slaughter of his captives for a whole year. ▷

30th November

Clarine's son rode in the Beautiful Forest until he came to an abbey, where he was told of the evil customs of Iweret, the best knight in the world. Whoever wished to challenge him had to strike the bronze cymbal which hung near a spring. Many had died here in the attempt. Nevertheless, Clarine's son rode and struck the cymbal: Iweret immediately appeared, and the two fought until Iweret was slain. Clarine's son was musing on his own prowess when one of the faery maidens from the Lake island appeared to him: 'Greetings in the name of my mistress. You have defended my lady's son and have overcome his enemy in fair fight. She therefore bids me name you rightly as Lancelot, the son of King Ban and Queen Clarine. Your rightful heritage is to be the best knight in the world.' And so it was that Lancelot gained a name, a lineage and renown in the passing of one day. Thereafter he journeyed to Camelot and was received by Arthur as a King's son.

▷ 16TH AUGUST

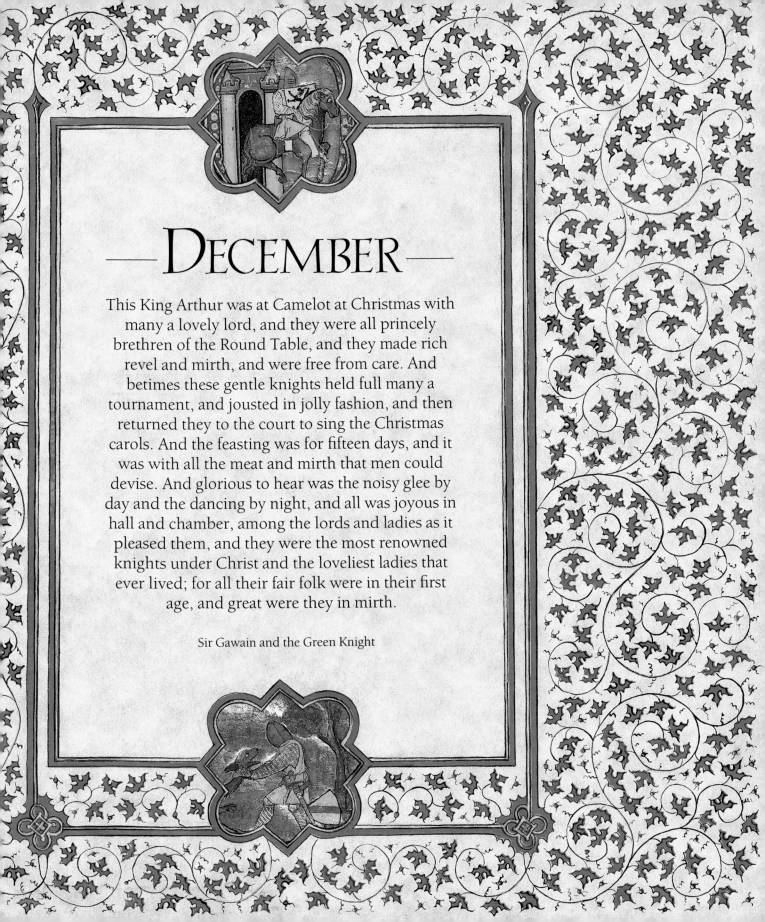

December

This King Arthur was at Camelot at Christmas with
many a lovely lord, and they were all princely
brethren of the Round Table, and they made rich
revel and mirth, and were free from care. And
betimes these gentle knights held full many a
tournament, and jousted in jolly fashion, and then
returned they to the court to sing the Christmas
carols. And the feasting was for fifteen days, and it
was with all the meat and mirth that men could
devise. And glorious to hear was the noisy glee by
day and the dancing by night, and all was joyous in
hall and chamber, among the lords and ladies as it
pleased them, and they were the most renowned
knights under Christ and the loveliest ladies that
ever lived; for all their fair folk were in their first
age, and great were they in mirth.

Sir Gawain and the Green Knight

1st December

One day as King Arthur rode hunting in the forest of Inglewood he became separated from his companions and found himself in a part of the forest he did not recognize. Suddenly he found that he could not move at all: his limbs were frozen. Then before him stood a menacing figure, dressed in night-black armour. 'Arthur, you are in my power,' a voice whispered in his ear. 'Unless you answer the question I shall ask, you will die.'

Arthur, finding his lips and tongue still free, asked: 'Who are you and what is this question you would have me answer?'

'I am Gromer Somer Jour, whose lands you took away and gave to Sir Gawain. If you would win your life return here in a year with the answer to this question: What is it every woman desires most?' Then he was gone, and the King found that he could move again. He returned to court chastened. ▷

2nd December

Arthur sought out Gawain and told him of the events in the forest. 'I will begin at once, my lord,' said Gawain. 'In a year I should find the answer.' And he set out along the roads, stopping every woman he met, noble or peasant, and asking her what she most desired. Soon he had a whole book, filled with different answers – but, somehow, none seemed right. ▷

3rd December

The year soon passed, and Gawain turned towards Camelot. Then he saw a woman sitting beside the road, dressed in a scarlet gown. She was the most hideously ugly creature Gawain had ever seen: her chin and her nose nearly met in the middle of her face, her eyes were odd colours and looked in opposite directions, her head was almost bald, and as for her body – it was so misshapen that she resembled nothing so much as a sack of kindling. As he came abreast Gawain was about to ride past. Then he hesitated – after all, she was a woman. Before he could open his mouth to ask the question she spoke: 'My name is Ragnall. I know what you are seeking, and I have the right answer. But only for a price.' 'What price is that?' Gawain asked. 'That you marry me.'

Gawain grew pale. But he said: 'If your answer is truly the one I seek, and is proven to be so, then I will agree to your terms.' And so when he entered the gates of Camelot that day Gawain had the hideous lady on his pillion. Few could bear to look her way, and all wondered at Gawain for allowing her near him. Arthur, too, frowned. 'I may not ask this of you, nephew.' But Gawain replied that they should wait for the outcome of the King's meeting with Gromer. ▷

4th December

Next day Arthur rode again in the forest, and as before he found himself facing Gromer Somer Jour. He gave the book of answers collected by Gawain to the black-clad knight, who gave them only a cursory glance before tossing them aside. Then he drew a black-bladed sword and raised it above Arthur. 'Wait!' cried the King – 'I have yet one more answer!' and he gave that of Ragnall. At once Gromer cried out in rage: 'Only my sister could have told you that. May she be cursed forever for her treachery.' Then he was gone, and Arthur returned to Camelot. There Gawain and Ragnall waited. Both could see that Arthur had triumphed. Gawain looked pale, Ragnall pleased. The wedding was set for the next day.   ▷

5th December

Despite the protestations of Guinevere, Ragnall insisted on a wedding feast with as many guests as could attend. Her table manners affronted everyone, as did her gross appearance in a white gown and veil. But soon enough the deed was done, the couple escorted to their chamber and left alone. There, Gawain gazed at the fire until his bride requested a kiss. Bravely, he assented, only to find that he held in his arms a radiant woman. 'How may this be?' he demanded. 'I was enchanted by my brother Gromer, forced to remain in that other shape until I found a man gentle enough to marry me. Now you have released me from part of the spell. Another part still exists. I can be fair by night and foul by day; or foul by night and fair by day. You must choose.'

Bewildered, Gawain thought. Then: 'I cannot make such a choice. It is for you to say.' And Ragnall clapped her hands for joy. 'Thus is the second part of the spell broken,' she cried, 'for you have given me the thing every woman most desires – freedom to be what she would be.' Thus Gawain married a fair bride, and lived happily with her.   ▷ 28TH MAY

6th December

There came to Camelot in the dark days towards the ending of the year a knight of Hungary named Sir Urry, who suffered from a terrible wasting sickness which had plagued him for years. He had all but given up hope of a cure when he heard of Lancelot's extraordinary prowess, and this had inspired him to make the long and difficult journey to Britain. 'Will you, Sir Lancelot, lay your hands upon me? For if you do so I shall surely be healed.' Lancelot turned away in anguish. 'If only I might do what you desire,' he said at last. 'But there are many knights far greater than I, and with more holiness.'   ▷

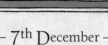

7th December

Sir Urry suffered many of the great knights who were at the court that winter to lay their hands upon him. But none made any difference. At last he begged again that Lancelot at least try what he might do. And so the great knight knelt beside the bier on which Sir Urry lay and prayed with all the fervour in his body that he might be allowed to help this poor, sick knight. He laid his hands upon his brow and slowly, slowly Sir Urry's face changed, the lines of suffering softened and he sat up. 'Now am I made whole through your goodness!' he cried, and many wept, Lancelot not the least, for the gift of this miracle to a sinful man.

8th December

There was no more generous man in the world than Sir Cleges. He kept open table for all and no one enjoyed the season of Christmas better than he. For ten years he had kept such lavish state at that blessed time that he had beggared himself and now, as Christmas approached once more, he mourned his poverty. He heard the minstrels practising their carols and looked upon the expectant faces of his children and wept. ▷

9th December

His wife, Dame Clarye, bade him be of good cheer and trust God. So it was that Cleges prayed earnestly to God and, as he prayed, the branch of a cherry tree landed on his head. He picked it up and found it covered with cherries and green leaves. Now it was the month of December, and Cleges ran to show his wondering household this great marvel. 'We shall take this as Christmas tribute to King Arthur,' he said. Dame Clarye hastened to make ready a basket and her husband set forth. ▷

10th December

When Cleges came to Cardiff, where Arthur's court was sitting, the porter looked upon his ragged clothes and refused him entry. But Cleges showed him the cherries in his basket. 'You shall give me a third of whatever the King gives you for these – in you go!' Cleges had the same difficulty with the usher and the steward, who each forbade him entry till they saw what was in the basket. To each of them, Cleges promised a third of whatever Arthur would give him. Everyone sat in hall waiting for the accustomed marvel which would herald the beginning of dinner. Cleges entered and presented the basket of cherries to Arthur. 'For this marvel', said Arthur, 'you may ask me whatever boon I can

grant.' 'Give me leave, lord King, to give twelve strokes to those who mocked me in your hall.' And Arthur was grieved at having to grant this. So it was that Cleges gladly granted a third of all that the King had given him to the porter, the usher and the steward in return for their discourtesy. Arthur called Cleges to him, 'For I believe that this knight was once a great and generous man. Good Sir Cleges, for your unselfishness in relinquishing so great a marvel and for the generosity of your largesse' – and here the court laughed at the discomfiture of the porter, the usher and the steward – 'I grant you this very castle of Cardiff and its titles and living.' And so Cleges and Clarye lived in great happiness and celebrated Christmas as they had been wont.

11th December

One day King Arthur and Queen Guinevere rode hunting in the forest of Inglewood, and when they had gone some way the Queen felt fatigued. So the King left her in the charge of Sir Lancelot and rode on, following the quarry. They rested by the lake known as Tarn Watheling, and as they sat a while and spoke of many things, the sky became dark and there came upon them a terrible spectre, yammering and shrieking out of the depths of the lake. Horrible to behold it was, with little flesh upon its bones, and long grey hair that clung to the skull like weed. As it neared them the Queen gave a terrible cry, for she recognized the ghost as that of her dead mother. Then a great fear came upon her, and even Sir Lancelot, who had faced many frightful demons in his time, grew pale and retreated before the spectre. 'Woe unto you, daughter,' cried the spirit, 'For you have committed a great sin, and for it you shall burn in Hell-fire for all eternity unless you repent and leave this evil thing.' And though the ghost named it not, yet did Sir Lancelot and the Queen know well that it was to their illicit love that it referred.

12th December

Arthur returned from the hunt bearing the White Hart's head. Now it had been the custom of the Pendragons that the head should be bestowed on the most beautiful woman in court, according to the King's choice. Guinevere had had a presentiment about this since she had received and forgiven Yder. She bade Arthur wait till Gereint returned to court, which he shortly did, bringing Enid with him. Guinevere dressed Enid in her own queenly raiment and led her down to the court. It was agreed by all present that Enid deserved the honour of the hart's head. Accordingly, Arthur presented it to the young bride and folded her into his kingly embrace, much to the discomfiture of Gereint. ▷ 24TH AUGUST

13th December

Morgain le Fay, for all her magic, and for all her great beauty, could not keep her lovers from straying. Thus she built a chapel in a valley and set about it a magic so strong that no faithless lover who set foot there could escape again, whence it came to be called the Valley of No Return. Many came that way and fell victim to its enchantments. This state of affairs might well have lasted forever, but that Sir Lancelot came there by chance, and by the power of his arm was able, because of his truly faithful love for Guinevere, to overcome the phantoms set to guard it, and to set free all the hapless knights who had been imprisoned there.

14th December

After he had banished Tristan, Mark thought long upon the punishment he would mete out to Isolt. It came to his ears that a group of lepers was in the area, and he devised the cruellest and most terrible revenge he could, declaring that his wife should be taken out, dressed only in a rough gown, and given into the hands of the leprous victims. But Tristan heard of this, and, disguising himself with a ragged cloak and leper's bell, secretly joined the company. When Mark's soldiers came and pushed Isolt from her mount in among the group of diseased people, Tristan came forward and, pretending salacious intent, seized her, allaying her terror by whispering that he was indeed Tristan and no leper. Mark's men rode off laughing and joking, but once they were gone from sight Tristan threw off his disguise and fled with Isolt to the one place where he deemed they would be safe – Joyous Gard, the home of Lancelot, who knew and sympathized with their case. And so the lovers came to find a haven of peace for a time.

▷ 1ST SEPTEMBER

15th December

Perceval found lodging in a fine castle. While he was waiting for dinner he noticed a splendid chessboard upon which were pieces of gold and silver. Before his startled eyes, the pieces began to move. He watched fascinated and decided to back the silver chessmen. The game played itself out to the end, but Perceval's pieces lost. In disgust, he heaved the whole chessboard out of the window into the lake. From the lake arose the apparition of his tutor in arms, the witch of Gloucester. 'Fine behaviour for a Round Table knight!' she scolded. 'That chessboard was the property of the lady of your heart, she who is Empress of the World. If you would win your quest, you must find it again and return it to this castle.'

▷ 25TH JANUARY

16th December

Morgain schemed to rid herself of her husband Uriens, to whom she had been married by the hated Uther Pendragon. The day came when she could no longer bear to see him alive, and she sent one of her maids to fetch Uriens' own sword. But the maid, seeing the madness in her mistress's eye, went and roused Sir Owain, who ran to his father's room in time to see Morgain raise the sword to kill him as he lay sleeping. Owain seized her from behind, crying out that she was mad. And as Uriens awoke Morgain threw herself at her son's feet, crying out that she had been possessed of a devil and knew not what she was about. And father and son took pity on her at that time, though soon Owain left for Arthur's court, while his father kept to his own chamber and saw little of his wife.

17th December

When Arthur had been long adventuring in the guise of the Knight of the Parrot, he boarded ship for Logres but was blown off-course to a mysteriously deserted land. On reaching shore, he saw a dwarf imprisoned in a high tower who stood crossing himself in amazement. It had been sixty years since the dwarf had seen another soul save only his son, a cannibal giant, who had placed his father in this tower for safety. Arthur was able to give the dwarf news of his native land, since he came from Northumberland, and to the dwarf's great joy he revealed himself as King Arthur.   ▷

18th December

Arthur heard the dwarf's story: how he had been voyaging with his pregnant wife, in the service of their lord. His wife's labour had been so arduous that their lord abandoned them there. The woman died and her boy had been suckled by a unicorn, who also brought meat for the dwarf. The boy grew prodigiously to his present size, but did not discriminate between the flesh of beasts and that of people, despite his father's remonstrance.   ▷

19th December

It was so that Arthur grew alarmed to see the giant boy return to the tower with food for his father. 'Will he not eat me?' he asked. The dwarf bade him lay down his arms and make no show of defence, if he wished to live. Arthur reluctantly did so, since strength of arms was useless. The dwarf spoke peaceably to his giant son, explaining that the knight was none other than King Arthur. The giant knelt in homage and promised to do all that the King commanded.

Lancelot suffers at the hands of Morgain le Fay in the Valley of No Return. All kinds of trials and tests face him, in the shape of dragons, spectral knights, a wall of fire, and a gigantic knight with an axe. (13th December)

To break the enchantments of Escalon the Dark, Lancelot opens a sealed door in the Perilous Chapel. He is attacked by invisible knights wielding swords and beats them off, but falls wounded before the altar. Owain and his damsel rush to revive him in the last frame of the picture. (26th December)

20th December

Queen Igrain was heavy with child. As the time grew near for her confinement, King Uther came to her and demanded to know whose child she bore. 'Sir,' said Igrain, 'the very night that my lord Duke was slain, there came a man to my bed. In every aspect he resembled Gorlois, and I loved him as a wife loves her husband. On that night I conceived the child I bear now.'

And Uther said: 'Be not afraid, my Queen. I am the father of your child.' And he told her the truth of that night's happenings, at which Igrain was glad, for she had feared for the safety of her unborn child.

Yet there were mutterings in the land. Some said that Uther married Igrain too soon after she was widowed for anyone to be sure whose child she carried. Yet they forbore to approach Uther directly about the matter, for they knew how fiercely he desired a son to establish his line.

In due time Igrain bore the child in the dead of winter, and it was a strong, healthy boy, at which Uther rejoiced greatly, so that now none dared speak to him of their doubts.

Then, when the infant was but a few weeks old, Merlin came before the King and reminded him of the great magic he had wrought that Uther might lie with Igrain in the likeness of her lord. 'I come now to claim my fee for this,' he said, and told Uther that he must be given the child. 'For I know well that there are those within your kingdom who doubt the parentage of the boy. Therefore let me take him to safe fosterage, where I can also watch him grow and see to it that he is guided in the ways of kings.'

Uther was silent for a long time, brooding, then at length he said slowly: 'Do you tell me that my son shall be king after me?'

'He shall be a far greater king than you, Uther Pendragon,' answered Merlin. 'Now give me the child.'

And so it was that in the darkness of the night Merlin took the boy, wrapped in a great purple cloak of Uther's, to a postern gate of the castle, and from then vanished into the land, so that none knew where he had gone. And Queen Igrain wept bitter tears, until Uther became yet grimmer of face, and gave out that the child had died. But Arthur – for so he was named – remained in hiding, as he grew to manhood.

▷ 10TH JANUARY

21st December

The year between the coming of the Green Knight and the time when Gawain must seek him out for a return blow passed all too quickly. Much of it was spent in searching for the Green Chapel. Everywhere Gawain asked, no one had heard of the place; or if they had, they spoke of it as a place of terror. As the year

turned towards winter the weather worsened. Gawain's course had taken him first north, then west, into the Wilderness of Wirral. There, exhausted, he found himself at the gates of a castle and begged shelter for the night. His host, a huge, vivid man who gave his name as Sir Bercilak, welcomed him warmly, reminded him that it was nearing the feast of Christmas, and urged him to remain there for as long as he wished. To Gawain's confession that he was in search of the Green Chapel, Bercilak replied that it was but three leagues distant, and that he could easily put him on the road for the place in a day or so, when he was rested. Gratefully, Gawain accepted the offer of warmth and food, firelight and gentle company. Within, he met the host's beautiful wife. He was made welcome, ate well and retired to rest in a comfortable bed with silken curtains. ▷

22nd December

Next day dawned bright and clear, and Sir Bercilak declared his intention of going hunting. He would not hear of Gawain accompanying him, however, but bade him rest some more after his arduous journey. 'Let you and me make a bargain,' he said, smiling. 'Whatever spoils I win today, let us exchange winnings for whatever you win here.' And he went laughing away to the noise of hounds and the calls of the horn.

After he had gone Gawain lay abed for a time, thinking of the Green Knight. Then in came the lovely Lady Bercilak, who sat on the end of the bed and made sweet talk with him. Courtier that he was, Gawain acquitted himself ably enough, and before the lady departed they exchanged a kiss. This became, when the lord returned, Gawain's only winnings, exchanged with bluff jesting for Bercilak's quarry of hares. ▷

23rd December

Next day was the same. Bercilak rode hunting again; his lady joined Gawain in his bedroom and made great verbal sport and play with him, ending with the exchange of two firm kisses. In the evening Bercilak returned with a great stag, and accepted Gawain's offering with hearty grace. ▷

24th December

The third day was the same, save that this time, after Gawain and the lady had exchanged three kisses, she drew from about her own waist a green baldric sewn with intertwining serpents of gold, and offered it to him. 'Whoever wears this will take no harm,' she said, 'No matter how strong the blow, he will

Sheltering in the castle of Sir Bercilak, Gawain is tempted by the lady of the castle as he lies abed preparing himself to face the Green Knight's axe.

be protected.' And Gawain, with his thoughts ever more upon the coming exchange with the Green Knight, took what she offered, though not without some misgiving. And that night, when Sir Bercilak returned, though Gawain gave up the three stolen kisses in exchange for that day's kill of a fine boar, he kept back the baldric, which he hid beneath his shirt. ▷

———— 25th December ————

Next morning, with Bercilak's careful directions in his head, Gawain rode until he came to a deep valley, between high ivy-covered banks. There he saw a cave mouth opening darkly into the depths of the hill, and heard the dreadful grinding of the axe being sharpened. Then the Green Knight himself appeared, every bit as terrible as before. 'Courteously do you return my pledge, Sir Gawain,' he said. 'Are you ready for the blow?' 'I am,' replied Gawain, feeling the green baldric against his skin. 'Strike clean. You shall not see a knight of the Round Table shake like any coward.'

The Green Knight raised his axe and brought it down, stopping a hair's breadth from Gawain's neck. 'I saw you quiver. Be still, man, and let me do my work!' Taking up his aim again he lifted the axe a second time, again stopping clear of Gawain's neck. This time Gawain did not move. 'That's better,' he said, 'you've got your nerve back.'

'Strike or be damned, I'll not flinch again!' cried Gawain.

The Green Knight hefted his axe a third time, and a third time brought it down so that it nicked the skin of Gawain's neck.

Gawain saw the trickle of blood on the snow. 'Now by heaven, I'll have done with this sport!' he cried, leaping to his feet. But the Green Knight merely smiled and said, 'Be of good cheer. The first stroke I withheld because you kept your appointment with me. The second stroke because you upheld your honour – although it didn't stop you accepting my pretty wife's kisses. But you deserved the third stroke because you accepted magical aid from her hands – that alone was unworthy.'

Gawain looked in astonishment at the Green Knight, under whose unearthly features he now recognized those of his cheerful host Sir Bercilak. 'How came you by this appearance?' he asked.

'Morgain le Fay enchanted me into this shape in order to test the honour of the Round Table. Now I am myself again. Return with gladness to King Arthur and tell of your adventure.'

When Arthur heard the story he decreed that Gawain should thereafter wear the green baldric in the form of a pentacle upon his shield, that all might know how courage strove with dishonour and won at the Green Chapel.

26th December

Owain and a damsel named Orisend summoned Lancelot to aid them in breaking the spell of Escalon the Dark, a knight whose dealings with necromancy had left the church where he was buried terribly haunted. When Lancelot came he forced open a door magically defended by swords, which attacked him of their own volition. The action of opening the door released the evil imprisoned within, but Lancelot fell fainting in the doorway. Owain and Orisend revived him and they gave thanks before the altar.

27th December

Queen Guinevere lived for another year after her lord had departed to Avalon, and only once more did she see Lancelot. He came to visit her after Camlan, with the news that was everywhere in the kingdom: of the final breaking of the Round Table Fellowship. And he pled with her to come with him to Joyous Gard, but Guinevere would not. 'The past is dead now, let it lie,' she said, and Lancelot left without another word. Then, a year later, he learned of her death, and went to pray beside her tomb, weeping for all the lost times and for the love they had shared despite everything.

▷ 9TH JUNE

28th December

One of Gawain's most terrible adventures was that of the Perilous Bed. He had arrived at a castle where his host seemed well disposed, and when night came he was shown to a splendid room in which was a great bed. Scarcely had he settled to sleep than a beautiful maiden slipped between the sheets. She laid a finger to her lips: 'Beware. You will be under attack as soon as you lay a finger on me.' So Gawain got his armour and weapons and touched the maiden – at which the bed began to roll about the room, while spears flew down from the ceiling. Gawain knocked them all aside and then went forth to do battle with his host, whom he soon slew. Then he returned to the bed and took the willing maiden in his arms.

29th December

Arthur bore long with the absence of Merlin. So intolerable was the depth of his loss that he sent to Blaise of Northumberland, who had been a sage much respected by Merlin and one who shared something of his wisdom. But Blaise's answer was mysterious: 'Seek not to disturb the falcon in his moulting cage. For as the eagle renews itself at the turning of the ages, so do the wise return in every

Gawain undergoes the test of the Perilous Bed, which moves of its own accord, while showers of arrows and spears and a fierce club-wielding giant attack him.

turning of the stars' procession. And as the Sleeping Lord shall come again, look then for the innocent youth who comes to set the kingdom right. Then shall the glass tower shatter and the Merlin fly forth renewed.' But Blaise spoke of ages yet to be and the meaning was obscure to Arthur.

30th December

*K*ing Arthur awoke from his long sleep, in which were many fevered dreams, and he rose and looked about him. Deep bowered and fair, the green landscape stretched away upon all sides. Sweet apple trees grew by the banks of a shallow stream, and white blossom was upon them like snow. But though the season should have been winter, the air was balmy and soft, and above, in the sky, the sun and moon shone forth together, and there were stars. Then Arthur knew that he was in Avalon, the Region of the Summer Stars, where rain and snow fall not, and where the great ones of the world await a call to arms. Smiling to himself, Arthur stretched his muscles and set off to walk by the stream, listening for the murmur of voices that would tell him that the Round Table was met again amid the trees.

> **HIC JACET ARTHURUS QUONDAM REXQUE FUTURUS**
> (HERE LIES ARTHUR, THE ONCE AND FUTURE KING)

EPITAPH TRADITIONALLY GIVEN TO ARTHUR, IN TOKEN OF HIS RETURN

31st December

*A*fter the death of Uther Pendragon the land of Britain knew no peace. Petty kings from every part of the country claimed the right to be High King over all, but none were strong enough to conquer all the rest. So Merlin devised a plan by which a new king should be chosen by no human agency. There appeared in the churchyard of the great Minster of St Paul in London a massive stone block upon which was set an anvil. Struck through the one into the other was a mighty sword, and in letters of gold around the stone was written: WHOSO PULLETH THIS SWORD FROM THIS STONE AND ANVIL IS RIGHTWISE KING BORN OF ALL BRITAIN.

When word of this got about, greedy men came from every part of the country to try and pull it forth. None succeeded. Then Merlin let cry a great tournament, to which all who wished might come and try their right to be king, and he made sure that Sir Ector, far off in the Forest Sauvage, knew of this, and had mind to bring his young sons, Kay and Arthur, to take part in the celebrations.

▷ 1ST JANUARY

THE CHRONICLE

The following chronology lists the stories in
the order in which they happened.

◇

The shields of some of the Knights
of the Round Table.

Arthur   Tristan   Gereint   Balan   Galahad   Perceval

Bedivere   Sagramore   Palomides   Mador de la Porte   Gawain   Kay

BIBLIOGRAPHY

Beroul: *The Romance of Tristan*, New York & London, Garland Publishing Inc., 1989

Bruce, James Douglas: *The Evolution of the Arthurian Romance* (2 vols), Gloucester, MA, Peter Smither, 1958

Butler, Isobel: *Tales From the Old French*, Boston & New York, Houghton Mifflin Co, 1910

Chrétien de Troyes: *Arthurian Romances*, trans. D.D.R. Owen, London, J.M. Dent, 1987

Cooke, Brian Kennedy: *The Quest of the Beast*, London, Edmund Ward, 1957

Der Pleier: *Meleranz*, ed. Kark Bartsch, Stuttgart, Litterarischer Verein, 1861

Der Pleier: *Tandereis und Flordibel*, ed. Ferdinand Khull, Graz, 1885

Geoffrey of Monmouth: *The History of the Kings of Britain*, trans. L. Thorpe, Harmondsworth, Penguin, 1966

Gottfried von Strassburg: *Tristan*, trans. A.H. Hatto, Harmondsworth, Penguin, 1967

Hall, Louis B.: *The Knightly Tales of Sir Gawain*, Chicago, Nelson Hall, 1976

Heinrich von dem Türlin: *The Crown*, trans. J.W. Thomas, Lincoln, Univ. of Nebraska Press, 1989

The High Book of the Grail (Perlesvaus), trans. N. Bryant, Cambridge, England, D.S. Brewer, 1978

Hill, Joyce, ed.: *The Tristan Legend: Texts from Northern & Eastern Europe in Modern English Translation*, Leeds, Univ. of Leeds, 1977

Jaufry the Knight & the Fair Brunissende, trans. Alfred Elwes, North Hollywood, CA, Newcastle Publishing Co, 1979

Karr, Phillis Ann: *The King Arthur Companion*, Albany, CA, Chaosium Inc, 1986

The Knight of the Parrot, trans. T.E. Vesce, New York, Garland Publishing Inc., 1986

Konrad von Stoffeln: *Gauriel von Muntabel*, ed. Ferdinand Khull, Graz, Leuschner und Lubensky, 1885

Lacy, Norris J., ed.: *The Arthurian Encyclopedia*, New York & London, Garland Publishing Inc., 1986

Lancelot of the Lake, trans. Corin Corley, Oxford University Press, 1989

Levi, Ezio, ed.: *Fiore di Leggende*, Bari, Laterza, 1914

The Mabinogion, trans. Lady C. Guest, London, David Nutt, 1902

Malory, Sir Thomas: *Le Morte DArthur*, New Hyde Park, NY, University Books Inc., 1961

Marie de France: *French Medieval Romances*, trans. E. Mason, London, J.M. Dent, n.d.

The Marvels of Rigomer, trans. T. Vesce, New York, Garland Publishing Inc., 1988

Matthews, Caitlín: *Arthur and the Sovereignty of Britain*, London, Arkana, 1989

Matthews, Caitlín and John, illus. Miranda Gray: *The Arthurian Tarot*, Wellingborough, Aquarian Press, 1990

Matthews, Caitlín and John: *Hallowquest: Tarot Magic & the Arthurian Mysteries*, Wellingborough, Aquarian Press, 1990

Matthews, John: *The Grail: Quest for the Eternal*, London, Thames & Hudson, 1981

Merlin (3 vols), ed. H.B. Wheatley, London, Early English Texts Soc., 1899

The Quest of the Holy Grail, trans. P. Matarasso, Harmondsworth, Penguin, 1969

Reiss, Edmund, Louise Horner Reiss and Beverly Taylor, eds.: *Arthurian Legend and Literature: An Annotated Bibliography. I: The Middle Ages*, New York & London, Garland Publishing, 1986

The Romance of Morien, trans. J. L. Weston, London, David Nutt, 1901

The Romance of Perceval in Prose, trans. D. Skeels, Seattle, Univ. of Washington Press, 1966

Schutz, James A.: *The Shape of the Round Table*,

Toronto, Univ. of Toronto Press, 1963
Sir Cleges and Sir Libeaus Desconus, trans. J.L. Weston, London, David Nutt, 1907
Sir Gawain and the Green Knight, trans. Rev. E.J.B. Kirtlan, London, Charles H. Kelly, 1912
Tarbe, Prosper, ed.: *Poètes de Champagne antérieurs au siècle de François Ier*, Rheims, Regnier, 1851
Ulrich von Zatzikhoven: *Lanzelet*, trans. K.G.T.

Webster, New York, Columbia University Press, 1951
Wace and Layamon: *Arthurian Chronicles*, trans. E. Mason, London, J.M. Dent, 1962
Way, G.L.: *Fabliaux or Tales*, London, Rodwell, 1815
Weston, Jessie Laidly: *Sir Gawain and the Lady of Lys*, London, David Nutt, 1907
Wolfram von Eschenbach: *Parzival*, trans. A.T. Hatto, Harmondsworth, Penguin, 1980

ACKNOWLEDGEMENTS

The authors acknowledge the kind assistance of all at Eddison Sadd who undertook to convey their vision to printed form, especially Amanda Barlow, the designer and illustrator. Thanks also to the following: Elisabeth Ingles, who bore so bravely the task of editing the manuscript; Elizabeth Eddison, for her sterling work in gathering the illustrations; Dick Swettenham for his timely translation of *La Puzella Gaia*; Prudence Jones for her support in the early stages of this project.

The quotations at the beginning of each month were translated as follows: January, December: by the Rev. E.J.B. Kirtlan; February, November: K.G.T. Webster; March: P. Matarasso; April: A.H. Hatto; June: D. Skeels; July: E. Mason; September: N. Bryant.

The authors and Eddison Sadd wish to acknowledge the museums and institutes which gave permission to reproduce the illustrations, as follows:

t – top; b – below; l – left

The Archbishop of Canterbury and the Trustees of the Lambeth Palace Library: p83, MS 6 f54v; p126, MS 6 f43v.

Bibliothèque Nationale, Paris:
p10, MS Fr 95 f159v; p13, MS Fr 118 f219v; p22t, MS Fr 342 f84v; p22b, MS Fr 12577 f18v; p29, MS Fr 113 f156v; p42, MS Fr 112 f239; p67, MS Fr 100 f50; p71, MS Fr 119 f312v; p72, MS Fr 122 f1; p77, MS Fr 99 f143; p86, MS Fr 343 f3; p90, MS Fr 343 f7; p95, MS Fr 115 f387; p130, MS Fr 343 f61v; p136, MS Fr 116 f667; p142, MS Fr 343 f59v; p158, MS Fr 95 f113v.

Bibliothèque Royale Albert 1er, Brussels:
p51, MS 9243 f49v; pp80–81, MS 9243 f39v; p111, MS 9243 f45.

The Bodleian Library, Oxford:
p17, MS Douce 178 f299r; p36, MS Rawlinson Q.b.6. f357; p44, MS Rawlinson Q.b.6. f384r; p56t, MS Douce 199 f70v; p64, MS Douce 199 f151v; p73, MS Rawlinson Q.b.6. f267r; p104, MS Douce 215 f14r; p118, MS Douce 178 f411v; p119, MS Douce 199 f221v; p121, MS Douce 383 f1; p132, MS Douce 178 f296v; p134l, MS Rawlinson Q.b.6. f246; p139, MS Douce 215 f39.

The British Library, London:
p14, MS Cotton Nero AX f94v; p16, MS Add. 12228 f202v; p27, MS Add. 17006 f8r; p34, MS Egerton 3028 f30; p40, MS Add. 10292 f3v; p61, MS Add. 10294 f45v; p93, MS Kay 15 Eiv f120; p116, MS Add. 38117 f185; p152, MS Add. 10294 f87v; p153, MS Add. 10294 f89; p154, MS Add. 10294 f90v; p156, MS Add. 10294 f94; p163, MS Add. 10294 f65v; p181, MS Cotton Nero AX f129.

Burgerbibliothek, Berne:
p184, MS Cod AA 91 (Parzival) f118.

Österreichische Nationalbibliothek, Vienna:
p38, MS 2537; p100, MS 2537; p107, MS 2737; pp113–114, MS 2537; p146, MS 2537.

The Pierpont Morgan Library, New York:
pp56–57b, MS 806 f253v; p97, MS 805 f48; p125, MS 805 f119v; p134b, MS 805 f109; p144, MS 805 f207: p148, MS 805 f99; pp178–179t, MS 805 f139; p178–179b, MS 805 f135.

Princeton University Library:
p122, Garrett MS 125 f37r; p138, Garrett MS 125 f52r; p165, Garrett MS 125 f40r.